Black Children and Poverty:
A Developmental Perspective

Diana T. Slaughter, *Editor*
Northwestern University

NEW DIRECTIONS FOR CHILD DEVELOPMENT
WILLIAM DAMON, *Editor-in-Chief*
Clark University

Number 42, Winter 1988

Paperback sourcebooks in
The Jossey-Bass Social and Behavioral Sciences Series

Jossey-Bass Inc., Publishers
San Francisco • London

Diana T. Slaughter (ed.).
Black Children and Poverty: A Developmental Perspective.
New Directions for Child Development, no. 42.
San Francisco: Jossey-Bass, 1988.

New Directions for Child Development
William Damon, *Editor-in-Chief*

Copyright © 1988 by Jossey-Bass Inc., Publishers
and
Jossey-Bass Limited

Copyright under International, Pan American, and Universal Copyright Conventions. All rights reserved. No part of this issue may be reproduced in any form—except for brief quotation (not to exceed 500 words) in a review or professional work—without permission in writing from the publishers.

New Directions for Child Development is published quarterly by Jossey-Bass Inc., Publishers (publication number USPS 494-090). Second-class postage paid at San Francisco, California, and at additional mailing offices. POSTMASTER: Send address changes to Jossey-Bass Inc., Publishers, 350 Sansome Street, San Francisco, California 94104.

Editorial correspondence should be sent to the Editor-in-Chief, William Damon, Department of Psychology, Clark University, Worcester, Massachusetts 01610.

Library of Congress Catalog Card Number LC 85-644581

International Standard Serial Number ISSN 0195-2269

International Standard Book Number ISBN 1-55542-885-1

Cover art by WILLI BAUM

Manufactured in the United States of America. Printed on acid-free paper.

Ordering Information

The paperback sourcebooks listed below are published quarterly and can be ordered either by subscription or single copy.

Subscriptions cost $60.00 per year for institutions, agencies, and libraries. Individuals can subscribe at the special rate of $45.00 per year *if payment is by personal check*. (Note that the full rate of $60.00 applies if payment is by institutional check, even if the subscription is designated for an individual.) Standing orders are accepted.

Single copies are available at $14.95 when payment accompanies order. (California, New Jersey, New York, and Washington, D.C., residents please include appropriate sales tax.) For billed orders, cost per copy is $14.95 plus postage and handling.

Substantial discounts are offered to organizations and individuals wishing to purchase bulk quantities of Jossey-Bass sourcebooks. Please inquire.

Please note that these prices are for the academic year 1988-89 and are subject to change without notice. Also, some titles may be out of print and therefore not available for sale.

To ensure correct and prompt delivery, all orders must give either the *name of an individual* or an *official purchase order number*. Please submit your order as follows:

Subscriptions: specify series and year subscription is to begin.
Single Copies: specify sourcebook code (such as, CD1) and first two words of title.

Mail orders for United States and Possessions, Australia, New Zealand, Canada, Latin America, and Japan to:
Jossey-Bass Inc., Publishers
350 Sansome Street
San Francisco, California 94104

Mail orders for all other parts of the world to:
Jossey-Bass Limited
28 Banner Street
London EC1Y 8QE

New Directions for Child Development Series
William Damon, *Editor-in-Chief*

CD1 *Social Cognition,* William Damon
CD2 *Moral Development,* William Damon
CD3 *Early Symbolization,* Howard Gardner, Dennie Wolf

CD4 *Social Interaction and Communication During Infancy,* Ina Č. Užgiris
CD5 *Intellectual Development Beyond Childhood,* Deanna Kuhn
CD6 *Fact, Fiction, and Fantasy in Childhood,* Ellen Winner, Howard Gardner
CD7 *Clinical-Developmental Psychology,* Robert L. Selman, Regina Yando
CD8 *Anthropological Perspectives on Child Development,* Charles M. Super, Sara Harkness
CD9 *Children's Play,* Kenneth H. Rubin
CD10 *Children's Memory,* Marion Perlmutter
CD11 *Developmental Perspectives on Child Maltreatment,* Ross Rizley, Dante Cicchetti
CD12 *Cognitive Development,* Kurt W. Fischer
CD13 *Viewing Children Through Television,* Hope Kelly, Howard Gardner
CD14 *Children's Conceptions of Health, Illness, and Bodily Functions,* Roger Bibace, Mary E. Walsh
CD15 *Children's Conceptions of Spatial Relationships,* Robert Cohen
CD16 *Emotional Development,* Dante Cicchetti, Petra Hesse
CD17 *Developmental Approaches to Giftedness and Creativity,* David Henry Feldman
CD18 *Children's Planning Strategies,* David Forbes, Mark T. Greenberg
CD19 *Children and Divorce,* Lawrence A. Kurdek
CD20 *Child Development and International Development: Research-Policy Interfaces,* Daniel A. Wagner
CD21 *Levels and Transitions in Children's Development,* Kurt W. Fischer
CD22 *Adolescent Development in the Family,* Harold D. Grotevant, Catherine R. Cooper
CD23 *Children's Learning in the "Zone of Proximal Development,"* Barbara Rogoff, James V. Wertsch
CD24 *Children in Families Under Stress,* Anna-Beth Doyle, Dolores Gold, Debbie S. Moscowitz
CD25 *Analyzing Children's Play Dialogues,* Frank Kessel, Artin Göncü
CD26 *Childhood Depression,* Dante Cicchetti, Karen Schneider-Rosen
CD27 *The Development of Reading Skills,* Thomas H. Carr
CD28 *Children and Computers,* Elisa L. Klein
CD29 *Peer Conflict and Psychological Growth,* Marvin W. Berkowitz
CD30 *Identity in Adolescence: Processes and Contents,* Alan S. Waterman
CD31 *Temperament and Social Interaction in Infants and Children,* Jacqueline V. Lerner, Richard M. Lerner
CD32 *Early Experience and the Development of Competence,* William Fowler
CD33 *Children's Intellectual Rights,* David Moshman
CD34 *Maternal Depression and Infant Disturbance,* Edward Z. Tronick, Tiffany Field
CD35 *How Children and Adolescents View the World of Work,* John H. Lewko
CD36 *Symbolic Development in Atypical Children,* Dante Cicchetti, Marjorie Beeghly
CD37 *Adolescent Social Behavior and Health,* Charles E. Irwin, Jr.
CD38 *Children's Gender Schemata,* Lynn S. Liben, Margaret L. Signorella
CD39 *Developmental Psychopathology and Its Treatment,* Ellen D. Nannis, Philip A. Cowan
CD40 *Parental Behavior in Diverse Societies,* Robert A. LeVine, Patrice M. Miller, Mary Maxwell West
CD41 *Children's Mathematics,* Geoffrey B. Saxe, Maryl Gearhart

Contents

Editor's Notes 1
Diana T. Slaughter

Part 1. Contemporary Perspectives on Socialization and Development

1. Cultural Diversity and Human Development 11
John U. Ogbu
Early formulations of environmental influences on human development have ignored the imperatives of cultural ecology.

2. Language Socialization 29
Shirley Brice-Heath
Environmental norms regulated by social class and race affect language socialization.

3. Patterns of Information Requests 43
William S. Hall, Elsa Bartlett, Alva T. Hughes
New patterns emerge from a naturalistic study of Black and White children's proactive language behavior in two social class groups.

4. Self-Concept Development 59
Margaret Beale Spencer
A critical review of two decades of research since the Moynihan report supports new theories about the development of Black children's self-system.

Part 2. Studying Black Children: Impact on Research and Social Policy

5. The Study of African-American Children's Development: Contributions to Reformulating Developmental Paradigms 75
Dalton Miller-Jones
Recent research in cognitive development shows how the study of Black children has influenced perspectives in the field.

6. Historical and Contemporary Linkages Between Black Child Development and Social Policy 93
Valora Washington
The study of Black children has encouraged the emergence of the field of child development and social policy.

Part 3. Epilogue

7. Black Children, Schooling, and Educational Interventions 109
Diana T. Slaughter
Implications of focusing on adaptive coping for schooling and related educational interventions with impoverished Black children are discussed.

Index 117

Editor's Notes

The idea of the Black underclass, according to Glasgow (1981), is the idea of substantial numbers of Black persons with little or no hope of ever obtaining the skills or resources necessary for upward social mobility in American society. In addition, these persons have difficulty meeting their basic needs for survival. They are unable to obtain work to support themselves or provide for their families. Glasgow (1987) has discussed three different perspectives on the origins of the Black underclass: the value deficiency perspective, the feminization of poverty perspective, and the social program perspective. He rejects each, arguing instead that structural factors in the American economy have created the social dislocation and marginality experienced by many Black workers in the past twenty to twenty-five years. Specifically, he argues that in today's post-industrial, service-oriented economy there are not enough job opportunities for unskilled laborers, an occupational category disproportionately held by Blacks. This view is shared by Wilson (1987).

From this perspective, neither the culture of poverty spreading across generations, the relatively high number of female-headed, single-parent families in Black communities, nor extended welfare dependency are significant single causal factors in the rise of the Black underclass.

This volume focuses on Black children in poverty or at risk of poverty by virtue of being members of families classified as the "working poor." Given the dire economic circumstances confronting Black children and youth, only the functional coping strategies of their families, particularly their extended families, buffer and protect children's early development. Therefore, it is especially important that we have an accurate account of the strengths and weaknesses of Black childhood socialization as revealed in the developmental and family research literature to date. Poverty, for example, has been a continuing factor in Black communities in America. What do we know about the resiliencies of Black children and families in relation to poverty? What aspects of Black culture, as engendered in the African-American experience, have buffered and protected children from the extremities and harshness of familial impoverishment?

The victims of poverty have always been negatively stereotyped in American society (Hamilton and Hamilton, 1986; Ryan, 1971; Sosin, 1986). Many Black parents have had to teach their children how to cope with the myths and stereotypes associated with the Black sociocultural heritage and economic status. How informative is today's developmental and socialization research on this important issue? Specifically, what gaps do we have in our knowledge base to date? Given the new economic

1

realities confronting both the nation and Black communities, what new data do we need? How applicable is information obtained over the twenty years since the Moynihan (1965) report to the future of Black children. Finally, what has been the impact of the research on the field of child development, both theoretically and methodologically, and does it support new standards and guidelines for research with children and their families?

Black Children and Poverty: A Persistent Relationship

Webster's *New World Dictionary* defines *minority* as "1. The lesser part or smaller number; less than half. 2. A racial, religious, or political group that is part of, but differs from, a larger, controlling group." The United States has a number of identifiable minority groups who are responsible for rearing children and who, by American standards, have a disproportionate number of impoverished families. Black Americans are one example. Other examples include members of some Hispanic communities (for example, Mexican American, Puerto Rican), diverse Native American groups, and some Anglo-Americans, including those living in relatively isolated rural communities. Newer minority groups at risk for poverty include recent Asian immigrant families, families living in formerly thriving industrialized regions of the nation, independent farm families in communities especially vulnerable to shifts in agricultural policies and practices, and families in households headed exclusively by women.

Child development researchers have infrequently addressed these populations in their studies. An important exception has been research on Black American children and families. In 1965, Moynihan published *The Negro Family: The Case for National Action.* He observed that, compared with White families, a disproportionate number of Black families were impoverished. Black families also had a disproportionate number of children failing in school, of adults marginal to the urban-industrial economy, and of single-parent households headed exclusively by women. Partly because of this report, social programs were initiated to assist poor children and families, many of whom were Black Americans. In the twenty-three years since the Moynihan report, many studies, both basic and applied, of Black child socialization and development have been conducted. Today, however, the phenomenon of Black children in poverty persists. Compared with White children, Black children continue to be disproportionately at risk of poverty.

A report, *Children in Poverty,* prepared for the Committee on Ways and Means by the Congressional Research Service (CRS) and the Congressional Budget Office (CBO) states: "Persistently poor children are overwhelmingly black, live in female-headed households, and live in southern or rural areas. Almost 90 percent of persistently poor children are black. About one-third of all children are poor sometime during childhood, but only one in twenty experiences persistent poverty. . . . Much of white poverty is short-term and associated with events such as divorce, remarriage, or changes in earnings. Black poverty lasts longer and is less affected by changes in family structure events. A higher percentage of black children than white children are born into poverty." (U.S. House of Representatives, Committee on Ways and Means, 1985, p. 54). These findings have been supported by a more recent report issued by the Select Committee on Children, Youth, and Families, *"Safety Net Programs: Are They Reaching Poor Children?"* Although pointing primarily to dramatic increases in poverty among White and Hispanic children between 1979 and 1984, the report states: "In 1984, black children continued to have the highest rate of poverty among the three racial/ethnic groups. However, over the five-year span, both the number of black children falling into poverty, and the rate of increase in the percentage of children in poverty for this group, was the lowest. . . . The poverty rate for black children rose from 40.8 percent in 1979 to 46.2 percent in 1984, or by 13 percent" (U.S. House of Representatives, Select Committee on Children, Youth, and Families, 1986, p. 4). The 1986 report includes dissenting minority opinions. Critics of the methods used to gather data for this report emphasize that the decision to sample by county and designate only percentages of impoverished children within each county for comparative purposes obscured the extent of the problem in densely populated, heavily Black, urban areas. Even this report, however, cites 1984 U.S. census data indicating that in the 1980s, nearly 50 percent of all Black children live in severely economically impoverished environments. (Comparable figures for Whites and Hispanics are 21 and 39 percent, respectively.) Fifty-one percent of Black children less than six years old live in poverty. (Comparable figures for Whites and Hispanics are 18 and 40 percent, respectively.)

The Psychosocial Impact of Persistent Poverty

If we assume that parental socialization for achievement motivation and educational attainment is greatly influenced by perceptions of children's future occupational prospects, and more important, by the lifestyle created by the family's own immediate participation in the labor force, then the change in available work greatly affects Black children's experiences in their early home environments. I predict that many children will observe and interact with adult family members who do not work and that the children will experience physical and psychological hardships associated with inadequate economic resources in the household. Some children from families with no adult workers will experience the defeatism, fatalism, and resignation felt by parents who have essentially given up hope of ever finding employment. In extreme instances, these children may live in families that depend on homeless shelters or even in families whose members are eventually dispersed because of the economic hardships. Other children will have parents with part-time, marginal, even seasonal, employment and will observe and experience the insecurities and frustrations of their primary caregivers. Many children will interact with adults who bear the sole responsibility for the household income. Particularly in urban areas, however, Black families need the income of two working parents to function adequately. Children will see that one full-time provider is necessary but not sufficient for the economic well-being of the entire family.

If we assume that persistent poverty establishes the basis for psychosocial stress with which an especially high proportion of Black children and families must cope, two important questions are raised by the findings of the preceding reports. First, what are the enduring effects of chronic poverty? Second, what naturally occurring, positive, adaptive coping strategies exist within Black American communities that support or can be developed to support positive coping?

The first question has a volatile history in academic and policy contexts. At one time, the effects of chronic poverty were assumed to be uniformly negative or bad, insofar as its victims were perceived as deficient, culturally deprived or disadvantaged, and generally lacking in psychosocial, economic, and material resources. It was impossible to imagine that the victims of poverty could have a viable, adaptive culture that had helped to sustain them, both individually and collectively, against great odds.

Discussions of poverty existing among Black children and families originated a generation ago. Initial discussions considered the impact of poverty as a form of psychosocial stress on parenting, language and cognition, self-concept, and family and school achievement. (See, for example, U.S. Department of Health, Education, and Welfare, 1968.) The pioneering efforts to conduct serious, scholarly research have contributed to researchers' knowledge of children, and childhood in general, in at least four topical areas highlighted in this volume: the impact of culture and community (cultural beliefs and attitudes) on family and child rearing; the relationships between culture and language socialization; the identity development of children; and cognitive development.

The theoretical impact of early efforts to conduct scientifically reliable and valid research with Black children has been to reformulate the developmental paradigm itself. Emergent emphasis on contextual theories of development; on descriptive, naturalistic methods; and on multivariate approaches to data analyses found persistent support from researchers who struggled to characterize the adaptive coping strategies used by low-income Black children and families to enhance the children's growth and development.

These contextually based theories and research findings have also affected structured programs designed to support the psychological and social development of poor Black children. One of the obvious areas that has been influenced is the study of family intervention and children's early development.

Further, because the ethnic and cultural heritage of Black children has been historically and uniquely affected by public policy, and because Black children are members of the largest American racial minority group, their status is an important indicator of American economic and social equity. Many believe that the advent of child development and social policy as an area of academic and scholarly focus can be partly traced to early efforts to link basic child development research to the real and applied experiences of low-income Black children.

Focus of This Volume

Given the aforementioned considerations, each chapter contributor was specifically informed that the purposes of this sourcebook are to (1) critically summarize important new knowledge in the contributor's research area—knowledge that was generated partly in an effort to understand better how poverty could potentially affect Black child development; (2) describe some of the theoretical and methodological redirections that were required to produce this new knowledge; and (3) speculate, given the research history, on future linkages between child development research and social policies that specifically address Black children and poverty. The chapter authors were invited to contribute because their research or writing areas are particularly salient to the sourcebook's theme of developmental perspectives on Black children and poverty. Each contributor, however, was free to emphasize one or more of the volume's specific goals according to that contributor's theoretical and methodological preferences in the field of child development research.

In Chapter One, John U. Ogbu emphasizes that culture should be defined to incorporate not just family or aspects of familial environments but also community environment and social norms. The anthropological perspective on culture shows how these environmental norms enter into processes of individual human development, such that different cultural tasks require socialization emphasis on different human competencies. Ogbu discusses how this theoretical analysis applies to the school achievements of African-American children.

Chapter Two, by Shirley Brice-Heath, discusses how natural community contexts influence early language socialization and behavior, particularly literacy development. The chapter begins with the research approaches and the model of socialization needed for appropriate consideration of the learning environments of Black homes and communities. Using her own fieldwork in a Southern community with Black middle- and lower-class families, the author discusses the similarities and differences between these two groups in their approaches to language usage and literacy. Implications for professionals, particularly Black professionals, who wish to improve Black children's school achievements, are discussed in the conclusion.

In Chapter Three, William S. Hall, Elsa Bartlett, and Alva T. Hughes report some important empirical data on children's information requests in Black and White, middle- and working-class home and school environments. Using methods from psycholinguistics and psychology, the authors describe linkages between race, socioeconomic status, and child-adult conversational interactions. The obtained findings do not always support notions of language deficits in lower-status children; in fact, children of working-class parents produced more information requests. The authors emphasize the importance of the situation (that is, topic, task, speaker-addressee relations) in discourse, thereby rejecting the idea of the language-deficient impoverished child.

Chapter Four, by Margaret Beale Spencer, reviews two decades of research and speculation on Black children's self-system since the 1965 Moynihan report. Several questions are explored: What is actually known and what remains a source of consistent misinterpretation or confusion in the literature? What have been some of the alternative conceptualizations or theoretical redirections required for determining real facts from unwarranted assumptions? What do we need to know? And, finally, what are the policy implications? The author points out that the research has consistently shown the independence of personal identity (for example, self-esteem, self-concept) and reference group orientation (for example, race identification, race awareness, racial attitudes and preferences) variables.

Dalton Miller-Jones, in Chapter Five, argues that psychological constructs prevalent during the 1950s and early 1960s encountered serious challenges when they were applied to African-American children. The chapter specifies how those challenges significantly channeled the direction of developmental theory and research and uses the study of cognition and cognitive development as a specific example. An attempt is made to establish greater continuity between the concepts and methods used today in the eighties and issues raised during, rather than before, the sixties.

In Chapter Six, Valora Washington examines some of the historical and contemporary linkages between Black children and social policy. She argues that the advent of the subdiscipline of child development and social policy itself can be traced to early efforts to link basic child development research to the experiences of poor Black children. However, despite the extensive use of statistics about Black children in policy contexts, the real needs and interests of Black children are still frequently obscured. As one example, plans to assist families and children, such as

Aid to Families with Dependent Children, are discussed from the perspectives of current policies as well as available, contraindicated Black child development research.

In Chapter Seven, the epilogue, I draw implications for developmental psychology and educational interventions, describing how recent developmental research has affected researchers' conceptualization of educational intervention and what the role of psychologists has been in that process. I conclude that renewed emphasis on the impoverished population need not necessarily be accompanied by a resurrection of refuted myths and stereotypes.

Diana T. Slaughter
Editor

References

Glasgow, D. *The Black Underclass: Poverty, Unemployment, and Entrapment of Ghetto Youth.* New York: Vintage Books, 1981.
Glasgow, D. "The Black Underclass in Perspective." In J. Dewart (ed.), *The State of Black America 1987.* New York: National Urban League, 1987.
Hamilton, C., and Hamilton, D. "Social Policies, Civil Rights, and Poverty." In S. Danziger and D. Weinberg (eds.), *Fighting Poverty: What Works and What Doesn't.* Cambridge, Mass.: Harvard University Press, 1986.
Moynihan, D. *The Negro Family: The Case for National Action.* Washington, D.C.: Office of Policy Planning and Research, U.S. Department of Labor, 1965.
Ryan, W. *Blaming the Victim.* New York: Random House, 1971.
Sosin, M. "Legal Rights and Welfare Change, 1960-1980." In S. Danziger and D. Weinberg (eds.), *Fighting Poverty: What Works and What Doesn't.* Cambridge, Mass.: Harvard University Press, 1986.
U.S. Department of Health, Education, and Welfare, National Institute of Child Health and Human Development. *Perspectives on Human Deprivation: Biological, Psychological, and Sociological.* Washington, D.C.: U.S. Government Printing Office, 1968.
U.S. House of Representatives, Committee on Ways & Means. *Children in Poverty.* Washington, D.C.: Government Printing Office, 1985.
U.S. House of Representatives, Select Committee on Children, Youth, and Families. *Safety Net Programs: Are They Reaching Poor Children?* Washington, D.C.: U.S. Government Printing Office, 1986.
Wilson, W. *The Truly Disadvantaged: The Inner City, the Underclass, and Public Policy.* Chicago: University of Chicago Press, 1987.

Diana T. Slaughter is associate professor in the Human Development and Social Policy Program of the School of Education and Social Policy at Northwestern University. She is currently a member of the Committee on Child Development Research and Public Policy of the National Research Council, National Academy of Sciences, and of the Board of Ethnic and Minority Affairs of the American Psychological Association.

Part 1.

Contemporary Perspectives on Socialization and Development

Students of human development in ethnic-minority cultures must ascertain the culture's repertoire of competencies and the indigenous formulas by which those culturally diverse competencies are socialized. Cultural attitudes toward schooling differ if the observed cultural diversity is based on primary or secondary cultural differences.

Cultural Diversity and Human Development

John U. Ogbu

What Is Culture and What Is Development?

Culture. Nonanthropologists studying human development and those involved in social policy and intervention programs tend to think of culture as what is in a person's immediate environment or family (Ogbu, 1987). Partly because their work focuses on people as individuals or in families and partly because of their perspectives on human functioning, they assume that culture consists of family environments or family characteristics. Sometimes community environment and social norms are considered cultural, but these elements are rarely included in discussions of development.

Culture is a way of life shared by members of a population (Ogbu, 1987). It is the social, technoeconomic, and psychological adaptation worked out in the course of a people's history. Culture includes customs or institutionalized public behaviors, as well as thoughts and emotions that accompany and support those public behaviors (LeVine, 1974). It includes artifacts—things people make or have made that have symbolic meaning. Particularly important is that the definition of culture includes people's economic, political, religious, and social institutions—the imperatives of culture (Cohen, 1971). These imperatives form a recognizable pattern requiring competencies that guide the behaviors of members of the culture fairly predictably.

Children develop as they mature, taking on their society's or group's customary behaviors, the thoughts and emotions that accompany and support such behaviors, knowledge and meaning of cultural artifacts, knowledge of societal institutions, and the practical skills that make the institutions work. Children acquire these cultural attributes because of maturational abilities, such as language, cognition, motivation, and empathy.

Students of human development, especially those oriented toward policy or intervention, tend to focus on the development of language, cognitive, motivational, and social-emotional skills. Unfortunately, these attributes are often measured and the results interpreted out of a cultural context. This problem can be avoided by using the notion of competence as a way of interpreting the developmental meaning of these attributes. Following Connolly and Bruner (1974), competence is defined as the capacity and the qualities that enable people to get things done in a manner considered appropriate by members of their culture. An example is the ability to speak a particular language in a way that members of a speech community find appropriate. From this point of view, child development can be defined as children's acquisition of the cognitive, communicative, motivational, social-emotional, and affective competencies characteristic of members of the culture to which the children belong, as well as the ability to use or manifest these attributes in a culturally appropriate manner.

Cultural Influences on Development. Culture influences human development by ensuring the physical survival of children (LeVine, 1974) and by ensuring that children acquire the cultural attributes of their society or population. In terms of conventional human development studies, culture influences development by ensuring that children acquire appropriate cognitive, communicative, motivational, and social-emotional or affective attributes, as well as the practical skills that will make them competent adults who will contribute to the survival of their society or population (Fishbein, 1976; Ogbu, 1981a). Finally, culture influences development by providing the formulas by which competencies are transmitted to and acquired by children. In this chapter I am not concerned with children's physical survival but only with their development of cultural competencies.

Psychobiological or Maturational Versus Cultural Outcomes of Development

To avoid the hereditists' problem (Jensen, 1969), we need to distinguish psychobiological or maturational outcomes of development from cultural outcomes of development. The two are not the same. An example of a maturational outcome is Piaget's idea of stages in cognitive development. The maturational outcome here is that of the individual's attainment of the final stage postulated by Piaget (1970), namely, the stage of formal operational thinking. In order to reach this final stage, a person's physical systems—the brain and central nervous systems—must be fully developed or matured for the kind of thought and language characteristic of the formal operational stage (Ginsburg and Opper, 1981).

No evidence exists that members of any known human population have failed to reach this physical systems maturity for operational thinking. Yet reports from cross-cultural studies indicate that populations vary in formal operational thinking (Dasen, 1977). In some populations, cultural tasks require a relatively high degree of formal operational thinking, and as a result this kind of thinking is valued and promoted. In other populations, cultural tasks do not call for much formal operational thinking, and it is apparently not highly valued and promoted. This distinction between psychobiological outcomes and cultural outcomes also extends to language, motivational, and social-emotional development.

Cultural Diversity and Development

Different cultural tasks require different competencies or different degrees of the same competencies. For example, pottery making seems to require and promote a greater ability to conserve a continuous quantity, such as clay, than fishing does. Bureaucracy as a cultural task appears to require and promote a greater ability to absorb complex information than subsistence farming does; bureaucracy may also require and promote a more formal operational thinking than subsistence farming does.

Members of different cultures are faced with different cultural tasks. In addition, the cultural tasks vary from culture to culture because different populations have worked out different solutions to common problems in life, such as how to make a living, reproduce, maintain order within their border, defend themselves against outsiders, and so on. The differences in solutions to the common problems arise from the fact that different populations live in different physical or different social environments that vary in resources. Furthermore, historical events that influence how people perceive and relate to their environment and how they perceive and relate to one another vary. Therefore, there are cultural differences in how to make a living (domain of economy and technology), how to govern (domain of polity), how to organize domestic life for reproduction (domain of family and child rearing), how to manage relationship with the supernatural (religious domain), and so on. Each domain both requires and promotes its own repertoire of competencies. Because the cultural tasks in a given domain (for example, subsistence tasks, tasks connected with domestic organization) differ cross-culturally, the repertoire of competencies or skills they require and promote also differ cross-culturally.

What children in a given culture develop or acquire as they mature physically are the competencies required and promoted by the cultural tasks of their society or population. These are the adaptive, that is, functional, competencies that parents and other child-rearing agents consciously or unconsciously value and promote. Because these competencies are used in rewarded tasks, they usually come to permeate other areas of life.

Consider, for example, cultural variation in the tasks of one domain of social life, namely, strategies for upward social mobility, which is related to achievement motivation. This variation is due to differences in historical and structural experiences, and it results not only in differences in culturally valued competencies but also in the way the competencies are transmitted and acquired. All human populations are biologically equipped for achievement motivation, as they are for language and cognition. Motivation, cognition, language, empathy, and other capacities are requirements for sociocultural adaptation at the hunter-gatherer stage of human evolution. However, beyond that stage, cultural differences in patterns of achievement strategies have emerged.

One pattern is well represented among White middle-class Americans. Among them, the culturally approved strategy for upward social mobility, or the strategy for getting ahead, stresses individual competition, drive, and initiative. These qualities are expected and rewarded at home, at school, and in the workplace. The same attributes permeate other domains of middle-class life, such as sports or recreational activities, politics, and even religion. The attributes also constitute an important part of the values underlying the child-rearing practices of White middle-class parents and other socialization agents. A second type of upward social mobility is found among the Lowland people in the Philippines. Here, in contrast to the American middle-class, interindividual cooperation is emphasized over competition: Competition occurs between groups rather than among individuals. Individuals achieve upward social mobility as a function of their success in building bonds with others and their participation in the group effort. The principle of cooperation and associated competencies permeate other domains of life, including subsistence economy, recreational activities, and religion. The socialization of children stresses cooperation, including the underlying beliefs, emotions, and competencies. A third form of getting ahead is found among the Kanuri of Northern Nigeria. The Kanuri expect aspirants for upward social mobility to attach themselves to and serve a patron. The aspirants will then be rewarded after they have demonstrated their "trust." This is done by showing the patron loyalty, obedience, servility, and compliance. These attributes permeate other domains of Kanuri life, including parent-child relationships, political relationships, and the like. To ensure that their children make it in the patron-client (aspirant) system, Kanuri fathers explicitly teach their sons how to become competent clients. For example, they instruct their sons to treat every relationship and interaction with superiors in the same manner the sons use with their fathers. Kanuri fathers even name their sons after potential patrons and encourage the boys to visit and serve such potential patrons from an early age. Eventually their services, loyalty, and trust are recognized and rewarded (Cohen, 1965).

In the area of cognitive competencies, the most fruitful work demonstrating cultural variation has come from studies of non-Western people. These cross-cultural studies are important not only because of their demonstration that variations in cultural outcomes are due to cultural differences in cultural tasks but also because of their methodological contributions. For example, Ciborowski (1979) suggests that to study the cognitive competence of members of a given population adequately, a researcher should first acquire a thorough knowledge of that culture, including knowledge of the cognitive competencies that are important to the members of the culture in their daily activities. It is not enough to search among members of the culture for the presence or absence of cognitive competencies the researcher considers important. The few cross-cultural psychologists who have succeeded in doing valid cross-cultural studies of cognitive competencies are precisely those who have followed the suggestion or observation of Ciborowski. These researchers have usually first gained a good knowledge of the indigenous activities and the associated competencies, the people's folk knowledge of and conceptual systems of what the people do, and then have proceeded to study the competencies used by the people in daily activities. Ciborowski cites a number of studies illustrating this approach (Price-Williams, 1961, 1962; Price-Williams, Gordon, and Ramirez, 1969; Lave, 1976; Posner, 1982; Saxe and Posner, 1983; Scribner, 1975, 1976; Gay and Cole, 1967).

Operating from somewhat similar assumptions that emphasize knowledge of the indigenous cultures and competencies, anthropologists and other scholars studying minority groups in the United States have shown that the competencies minority children acquire or develop in the community are often different from the competencies the children are required to demonstrate at school. Furthermore, these researchers have shown that because the competencies minority children bring to school are different from those required at school, the children encounter conflicts in competencies that cause adjustment and learning difficulties. For example, some studies have found that Blacks and other minorities have different cognitive styles as compared with the style on which school learning is based. Blacks speak a dialect of English rather than the standard English, and in a Native American community studied by Philips (1972, 1983), communicative competence is not defined in the same way that it is defined at school. In a study of classrooms serving Native American students, Erickson and Mohatt (1982) found that the social interaction pattern of the Native Americans was different from the pattern of conventional social interaction in the school. The studies by Philips show clearly that minority children have already been socialized into the competence of their community by the time they begin school and confront a different kind of competence—the competence of the school.

Cultural Formulas for Producing Cultural Outcomes of Development

I noted earlier that the hereditists' problem is that they fail to distinguish psychobiological outcomes of development from cultural outcomes of development. The environmentalists' problem is that they fail to differentiate the processes or formulas by which a culture ensures that the culture's children will acquire appropriate competencies by the time the children grow up from the cultural factors that caused the competencies to exist in the culture as necessary attributes of its members. The environmentalists' problem has its root in a Western middle-class-centric view of development. This view assumes first that, in the course of the evolution of human competencies, those of the Western middle class emerged as the highest form and the ideal against which the competencies of other populations must be measured and second that Western middle-class competencies are what they are because of Western middle-class child-rearing practices (White, 1979). Both assumptions are, of course, erroneous because, as stated before, population differences in competencies are due to differences in the cultural tasks that require the competencies rather than to differences in child-rearing practices. Moreover, as discussed in the next section, when a people's culture changes, or when they emigrate to other cultures, they acquire the competencies required by the cultural tasks that confront them in the new situation, even though they were not raised as children under the new condition or in the same way as members of the new, host culture.

There are, therefore, two ways by which people in a culture acquire the competencies prevalent in the culture—that is, competencies they need in order to become competent members of the culture. One is by participating as children or as adults in the cultural tasks that require the competencies. As I have stated, this seems to be the method by which immigrants acquire the competencies prevalent in their host society, and it is the method by which people undergoing cultural change acquire the competencies required by the emergent cultural tasks.

The other way is through cultural formulas for raising children that have been developed by a particular population over time. Again, members of a population usually come to value the competencies that make them successful in cultural tasks that are rewarding, and this influences how they try to raise their children. Depending on their overall understanding of the situation, they may deliberately teach their children the competencies the parents themselves have found useful. Then, as the children get older they, too, may actively seek to acquire those same skills. For example, potters will teach their children pottery making and the competencies needed to be successful at pottery making, and potters' children will eventually seek to learn how to make pottery. Likewise, subsistence farmers will teach their children subsistence farming skills (Ruddle and Chesterfield, 1977). The farmers will not teach their children how to be successful urban wage earners, and unless influenced by urbanization and other factors, the farmers' children will strive to learn to be successful subsistence farmers.

Whatever may be the desired form of cultural outcomes—cognitive, communicative, and social-emotional—members of a culture usually have culturally approved formulas or practices for developing these competencies in children through early experience and beyond. The formulas consist of teaching the children directly and indirectly, consciously and unconsciously, the instrumental competencies and supportive beliefs and emotions already existing in the population that parents and other socialization agents know that the children will need as adults to perform cultural tasks. Parents in each generation do not invent the knowledge, beliefs, competencies, and behaviors that they teach their children. These already existed, except in a period of social change. Thus, even in the contemporary United States, the competencies that the middle class foster in their children, such as self-direction, initiative, independence, competitiveness, and certain cognitive and communicative skills (Connolly and Bruner, 1974; Kohn, 1969; Leacock, 1969; Ogbu, 1981b, 1987; Vernon, 1969), are not the invention of present-day middle-class parents. Rather, today's middle-class parents stimulate their children to develop the attributes that generations of the White middle class have found were adaptive for their high-level, high-paying occupations and other social positions (see also Seeley, Sims, and Loosely, 1956). Parents in a hunting and gathering society and parents in a peasant community value and teach their children other types of competencies that are more adaptive for their children's particular cultural tasks.

The formulas work because parents and other socialization agents use culturally standardized techniques of child rearing that time and experience have shown to be effective in producing the desired cultural outcomes of development. However, in contemporary urban-industrial societies like the United States, some cultural brokers, known as child developmentalists, have emerged. These experts are cultural functionaries in a constantly changing culture. Their culturally sanctioned task is to study changes in middle-class cultural tasks, especially tasks in the techno-economic domains, and to devise and disseminate appropriate changes in child-rearing formulas to enable middle-class parents to transmit new competencies required by the changing cultural tasks (Ogbu, 1981a, 1987).

Cultural Diversity, Development, and Change

Although people develop or acquire the cognitive, communicative, motivational, social-emotional, and other competencies of their culture during their formative years, these attributes can change when people undergo culture change. A common cross-cultural observation is that when people's cultures change, bringing about new cultural tasks, people usually learn or develop the new competencies required by the cultural tasks that now face them. The Western middle class is an example of a population whose competencies have changed because of culture change. Both Baumrind (1976) and Vernon (1969) suggest that the development of a bureaucratic urban-industrial economy in the West gave rise to the modern Western pattern of thinking skills. Industrialization, urbanization, bureaucratization, and increased formal education, according to Vernon, produced new cultural tasks that required and promoted new skills for absorbing complex information, manipulating abstract concepts, and grasping relations. These skills were initially used to solve specific problems at school and in the workplace, but they eventually came to permeate the daily activities of the middle class.

Apparently, further changes are occurring today in the cognitive skills of the middle class because of computer and related technologies. These skills emphasize precision in thinking and related rules for critical thought, according to a report of the Committee of Correspondence on the Future of Public Education (1984). Middle-class Americans are acquiring the new cognitive competencies by learning to use computers at home, school, and work; they are modifying their child-rearing practices and children's education to enable their children to acquire the new cognitive competencies. American schools, too, are deliberately promoting the new competencies by rewriting their curricula and teaching methods under public pressures to emphasize the new skills compatible with computer thinking and with other emerging cultural tasks that rely on computer and new technological know-hows.

Evidence of change in competencies as a result of culture change also can be found in Third-World countries. As Third-World people come under the influence of Western technology and participate in new cash economy, bureaucratic organizations, urbanization, and Western-type schooling, they appear to be undergoing a kind of cognitive acculturation. They are increasingly acquiring or developing cognitive competencies similar to those of the Western middle class, including competencies for absorbing complex information, for manipulating abstract concepts, and for grasping relations. They are also acquiring new language and communicative competencies for bureaucratic and related tasks (see Cole, Gay, Glick, and Sharp, 1971; Cole and Scribner, 1974; Seagrim and Lendon, 1980; Sharp, Cole, and Lave, 1979; Stevenson, 1982).

Emigration provides yet another instance in which people who undergo change develop new competencies. Immigrants find it necessary to learn to communicate, to think, to interact, and to strive for self-betterment the way members of their host culture do. They may retain some of the competencies of their homeland, but, in a generation or two, they and their descendants usually come to be characterized by new cognitive, communicative, motivational, and behavioral attributes sufficient enough to differentiate them from their peers back home. However, not all instances of contact with a new culture result in changes in competencies. The case of minorities in contemporary urban-industrial societies illustrates instances of both change and nonchange, and this calls for a reexamination of the meaning of cultural diversity.

Minority Status, Cultural Diversity, and Human Development

In the United States, minority groups, such as Native Americans, Black Americans, Chinese Americans, Mexican Americans, and Puerto Ricans, have their own cultures, language, and dialects. However, this cultural diversity is not reflected in studies of human development in these populations. That is, researchers do not start from a good knowledge of the minority cultures. They do not study the minorities' indigenous activities, folk knowledge, and conceptual systems and then use this knowledge to ascertain the skills or competencies the minorities use in the activities that their children must develop to function as competent adults in their culture.

On the contrary, students of human development in minority populations operate from more or less the middle-class-centric point of view described earlier. Thus, researchers design their studies to determine the extent to which members of the minority populations use White middle-class child-rearing practices and develop White middle-class competencies. Often they conclude that the minorities failed to develop the White middle-class competencies to an acceptable degree because minority parents did not use White middle-class child-rearing practices. This approach is well illustrated by studies purporting to measure the development of thinking skills of minority children about how to resolve interpersonal conflicts and of the children's strategies for resolving such conflicts. The researchers' approach to this problem has been primarily from their knowledge of how White middle-class children think and what these children do about interpersonal conflicts in the school setting. On the basis of this knowledge, researchers have constructed tests to measure the developmental levels of minority children and to evaluate the capability of minority parents to raise their children to develop adequately.

The research of Shure, Spivack, and associates is a case in point (Shure, Spivack, and Jaeger, 1971; Shure, Spivack, and Gordon, 1972; Shure and Spivack, 1979; Shure and Spivack, 1980). These researchers assumed that White middle-class children adjust well in school—that is, these children do not fight or disrupt classes in other ways because of their conceptual and practical skills in resolving interpersonal conflicts. The White middle-class competencies include ability to think up a variety and range of alternative solutions for resolving a conflict. Examples of children's interpersonal conflicts are those that arise when a child wants a toy held by another child and those that arise when a child breaks something that belongs to another child. Alternative resolutions of such conflicts might include using the teacher as a mediator, negotiating with the other child, and fighting over the item. The cognitive or thinking skills involved would include conceptualizing the alternative solutions, recognizing potential outcomes or consequences of each solution, and thinking in terms of cause and effect.

In several studies, Shure and her associates administered batteries of tests to lower-class Black children, and in some cases to middle-class White children, to assess the children's development of the thinking skills used for problem solving. The general finding was that lower-class Black children do not think about resolving interpersonal conflicts the same way the middle-class White children think about resolution, nor do Black children go about resolving their conflicts the way their White peers do. The researchers then interpreted the differences as evidence that lower-class Black children are deficient in their development of competencies for resolving interpersonal conflicts. They also implied that this developmental deficiency was the result of faulty early socialization and that it contributed to disruption in the classroom.

I cannot accept the conclusion of these studies, namely, that lower-class Black children are deficient in developing thinking skills for resolving interpersonal conflicts and that this deficiency occurs because Black parents do not use the child-rearing practices used by White middle-class parents. It is possible that the lower-class Black culture has its own repertoire of thinking skills for resolving interpersonal conflicts and its own set of strategies for dealing with such conflicts. The investigators did not study the indigenous knowledge and strategies that Black parents and other socialization agents fostered in the children and that the children strove to acquire as the children matured.

Perhaps one major reason why studies of human development in minority populations have not paid attention to the minorities' own cultural competencies and practices is that the studies have been conducted in connection with policies and intervention programs. That is, the studies have been based on the middle-class-centric assumptions discussed earlier and have been intended to provide a rationalization for teaching disadvantaged or at-risk children the proper, middle-class competencies. For example, a major intervention effort intertwined with studies in the development of low-income Black children has been to raise the Black children's IQ through programs that exposed them to presumed early experience of white middle-class children. Although such intervention efforts have been made through parent education and preschool education, they have not been particularly successful in inoculating minority children against future school failure and related problems. As pointed out elsewhere (Ogbu, 1978, 1981b, 1985), these intervention approaches are not particularly successful because they are based on theories and research designs that err in their assumptions about origins of human competencies, particularly origins of minority children's competencies.

Yet it is not enough to recognize that minorities have their own cultures with indigenous activities, conceptual systems, and the like. Mere cultural differences among the minorities do not account for their differences in school adjustment and academic performance. Some minorities do quite well in school, even though they have their own culture and language or dialects and even though they do not use the child-rearing practices of the White middle class. Other minorities who also have their own cultures and languages and do not use the White middle-class child-rearing practices do less well in school. Thus, it seems that some cultural diversity permits the minorities to cross cultural boundaries and do well in school, whereas some other cultural diversity discourages the minorities from crossing cultural boundaries. Let us briefly examine the two types of cultural diversity, starting with the types of minorities with which they are associated.

I have designated one as *primary cultural differences* and the other as *secondary cultural differences* (Ogbu, 1982). Primary cultural differences are those that existed before two populations came in contact. Persons who have these differences can cross cultural boundaries and are found among immigrant minorities in the United States and among non-Western people attending Western-type schools in their own societies. Take the case of Punjabi immigrants in Valleyside, California. Before they emigrated to the United States, the Punjabis practiced Sikh, Hindu, or Moslem religion, had arranged marriages, and the males wore turbans. They also had their own way of raising children, including training children in decision making and money management. To some extent, the Punjabis still do these things in the United States. They try to keep some aspects of their native culture, but they also try to learn features of American mainstream culture and language and to acquire the White middle-class competencies they perceive they need to achieve the goals of their emigration (Gibson, 1988).

Several factors enable bearers of primary cultural differences to cross cultural boundaries to acquire new cognitive, communicative, motivational, and social-emotional competencies that, in turn, help them succeed in school and later in the workplace. One is that the primary cultural differences are associated with immigrant minority status. Immigrant minorities are people who have moved more or less voluntarily to the United States because they believed that this would lead to greater economic well-being, better overall opportunities, and/or greater political freedom. These expectations continue to influence the way immigrants perceive and respond to cultural, language, and other differences they encounter and to schooling. Moreover, the immigrants see the cultural and language differences they encounter or brought with them as barriers to be overcome to achieve the goals of their emigration. So they make concerted efforts to learn, and they encourage their children to acquire standard English and the cognitive, motivational, and social-emotional competencies that enhance success in school and in the workplace. Still another factor enabling bearers of primary cultural differences to cross cultural boundaries is that the cultural differences did not develop in opposition to White American culture, that is, as coping mechanisms under subordination. Therefore, the immigrants do not equate the acquisition of attributes that enhance success in school with the acquisition of White American culture; nor do they perceive school learning as threatening to their own minority culture, language, and identity.

Secondary cultural differences, on the other hand, are differences that arise after two populations have come in contact with each other or after members of one population have begun to participate in the schools or other institutions controlled by members of another population. In other words, secondary cultural differences develop as a response to a contact situation, especially one that involves the subordination of one population by another. Such subordination is usually associated with castelike or involuntary minority status.

Involuntary minorities are people who were initially brought into the society of the United States involuntarily through slavery (as in the case of Black Americans) or conquest (as in the case of Native Americans and of Mexican Americans in the southwestern United States). After their involuntary incorporation, these minorities were relegated to menial positions, given discriminatory instrumental and expressive treatments, and denied true assimilation into the mainstream society. Involuntary minorities do not interpret their presence in the United States as a longed-for opportunity to improve their status. Rather, they resent their enforced incorporation and their lost golden age and generally feel that their dismal future cannot be improved without collective struggle.

Although during the incorporation period, the minorities and White Americans were each characterized by primary cultural differences, the minorities began to develop secondary cultural differences after that initial phase as they attempted to cope with their treatment by Whites. The new development in the minority cultures involved partly reinterpretations of their primary cultural differences and partly the development of new cultural forms and behaviors.

A comparative analysis indicates specific features that distinguish secondary cultural differences from other forms of cultural differences. One is that secondary cultural differences tend to emphasize differences in style rather than in content, as in the case of primary cultural differences. Researchers have located the differences in style with respect to cognitive competencies (Ramirez and Castenada, 1974; Shade, 1982), communication (Gumperz, 1981; Kochman, 1982), social interaction (Erickson and Mohatt, 1982), and learning (Au, 1981; Boykin, 1980; Philips, 1976). The second feature is cultural inversion (Holt, 1972; Ogbu, 1981a). This is the tendency for the minorities to regard certain forms of behavior, events, symbols, and meanings as inappropriate because they are characteristic of White Americans. At the same time, the minorities claim other (often the opposite) forms of behavior, events, symbols, and meanings as appropriate because these are *not* White ways. Thus, what is appropriate or even legitimate for in-group members is defined in opposition to the preferences and practices of White Americans in selected domains of life. This results in a kind of coexistence of two opposing cultural frames of reference, one appropriate for the minorities and the other for White Americans. Closely associated with the oppositional cultural frame of reference is the development by the minorities of a kind of oppositional social identity with regard to the White American social identity. A fourth characteristic is that secondary cultural differences may embody a folk theory of getting ahead that differs in some important respects from the White middle-class folk theory of getting ahead through formal educational credentials. Still another characteristic of secondary cultural differences is a pervasive distrust of White Americans.

Whether the case is that of Native Americans, the original owners of the land who were conquered and shoved into reservations, or that of Black Americans brought from Africa as slaves, it is evident that these minorities have developed secondary cultural differences or coping mechanisms to deal with the economic, political, psychological, and social problems they faced collectively after their involuntary incorporation into American society. Sometimes the coping mechanisms are overt opposition; sometimes they are covert.

It is more difficult for bearers of secondary cultural differences, that is, involuntary minorities, to cross cultural boundaries because of the way they interpret their history and assess their situation in the United States, because of their folk theory of getting ahead and the resulting alternative or survival strategies they have developed, because of their oppositional cultural frame of reference and social identity, and because of their distrust of White Americans and White American institutions. Consider the problems raised by the oppositional process. Because secondary cultural differences arose from a need for involuntary minorities to cope with the problems of economic, social, and other forms of subordination and to maintain their sense of self-worth, these minorities, in contrast to immigrant minorities, do not interpret the cultural differences they encounter in school and society as barriers to be overcome. Rather, involuntary minorities see these cultural differences as symbols of identity to be maintained. Thus, involuntary minorities may negatively, albeit unconsciously, sanction or oppose speaking the standard English because it is White. A related contrasting problem is that the immigrants may lack certain competencies necessary to do well in school because their own cultures did not include or promote such competencies. Nevertheless, the immigrants recognize this and then try to learn the missing competencies. Involuntary minorities, on the other hand, may have the competencies needed to do well in school but may use them in a different way or style that they resist changing because it symbolizes their identity.

Furthermore, involuntary minorities tend to equate school learning with learning a White American cultural frame of reference that they may also see as taboo. Therefore, school learning itself or the learning of the competencies that enhance school success may be perceived, albeit unconsciously, as a threat to the minorities' culture, language, and identity. The learning may be censored by peers, but it also may be censored by self. With regard to self-censorship, DeVos (1984) suggests that, in a situation involving an oppositional process, a member of an involuntary minority may automatically or unconsciously perceive learning things identified with those considered oppressors as harmful to the member's identity. Learning in such a situation tends to arouse a sense of impending conflict over the member's future identity. Of course, not every member of an involuntary minority group feels this way (Fordham and Ogbu, 1986; Ogbu, 1987, in press). A final disincentive for learning or expressing competencies associated with White Americans and their institutions is the tremendous distrust that involuntary minorities have for Whites and the schools and other institutions Whites control.

What does all this mean for research in human development among minority populations? It means that the researcher not only must start from a thorough knowledge of the minority culture in order to ascertain what type of cultural diversity is involved—diversity based on primary cultural differences or diversity based on secondary cultural differences.

Conclusion

Culture plays a crucial role in human development and education, but the role of culture is complex and not yet well understood. In human development studies, cultural outcomes need to be distinguished from psychobiological or maturational outcomes. Hitherto, research on development in minority populations has not made this kind of distinction. Usually, the implication is that the White middle-class developmental outcomes and processes are to be expected of the non-White minorities. Comparative studies outside the United States show that developmental outcomes vary in different populations and that the differences in outcomes are due to differences in cultural tasks and cultural requirements. A further complication arises from a comparative analysis of the school adjustment and academic performance of minority groups whose cultural backgrounds are different from those of the White middle class. This analysis shows that the differences found are not due to mere differences in culture or in outcomes of development. The relationship between culture, development, and school performance seems to be more complex in that it involves historical, structural, and psychological or expressive factors not ordinarily considered by students of human development. Yet probing and understanding this complex relationship will lead to better interpretation of research findings, which, in turn, can form the basis for a better social policy.

References

Au, K. U. "Participant Structure in a Reading Lesson with Hawaiian Children: Analysis of a Culturally Appropriate Instructional Event." *Anthropology and Education Quarterly*, 1981, *10* (2), 91–115.

Baumrind, D. "Subcultural Variations in Values Defining Social Competence: An Outsider's Perspective on the Black Subculture." Unpublished manuscript, Institute of Human Development, University of California, Berkeley, 1976.

Boykin, A. W. "Reading Achievement and the Social-Cultural Frame of Reference of Afro-American Children." Paper presented at NIE Roundtable Discussion on Issues in Urban Reading, Washington, D.C., November 19–20, 1980.

Ciborowski, T. J. "Cross-Cultural Aspects of Cognitive Functioning: Culture and Knowledge." In A. J. Marsella, R. G. Tharp, and T. Ciborowski (eds.), *Perspectives on Cross-Cultural Psychology*. San Diego: Academic Press, 1979.

Cohen, R. "Some Aspects of Institutionalized Exchange: A Kanuri Example." *Cashiers d'Etudes Africaines*, 1965, *5* (3), 353–369.

Cohen, Y. A. "The Shaping of Men's Minds: Adaptations to the Imperatives of Culture." In M. L. Wax, S. Diamond, and F. O. Gearing (eds.), *Anthropological Perspectives on Education*. New York: Basic Books, 1971.

Cole, M., Gay, J., Glick, J. A., and Sharp, D. W. *The Cultural Context of Learning and Thinking: An Exploration in Experimental Anthropology*. New York: Basic Books, 1971.

Cole, M., and Scribner, S. *Culture and Thought: A Psychological Introduction*. New York: Wiley, 1974.

Committee of Correspondence on the Future of Public Education. *Education for a Democratic Future: A Manifesto.* New York: Committee of Correspondence on the Future of Public Education, 1984.

Connolly, K. J., and Bruner, J. S. "Introduction." In K. J. Connolly and J. S. Bruner (eds.), *The Growth of Competence.* San Diego: Academic Press, 1974.

Dasen, P. (ed.). *Piagetian Psychology: Cross-Cultural Contributions.* New York: Gardner Press, 1977.

De Vos, G. A. "Ethnic Persistence and Role Degradation: An Illustration from Japan." Paper presented at the American-Soviet Symposium on Contemporary Ethnic Processes in the USA and the USSR. New Orleans, April 14–16, 1984.

Erickson, F., and Mohatt, G. "Cultural Organization of Participant Structure in Two Classrooms of Indian Students." In G. D. Spindler (ed.), *Doing the Ethnography of Schooling: Educational Anthropology in Action.* New York: Holt, Rinehart & Winston, 1982.

Fishbein, H. D. *Evolution, Development, and Children's Learning.* Pacific Palisdes, Calif.: Goodyear, 1976.

Fordham, S., and Ogbu, J. U. "Black Student's School Success: Coping with the 'Burden of Acting White.' " *The Urban Review,* 1986, *18* (3), 176–206.

Gay, J., and Cole, M. *The New Mathematics and an Old Culture: A Study of Learning Among the Kpelle of Liberia.* New York: Holt, Rinehart & Winston, 1967.

Gibson, M. A. *Accommodation Without Assimilation: Punjabi Sikh Immigrants in an American High School and Community.* Ithaca, N.Y.: Cornell University Press, 1988.

Ginsburg, H., and Opper, S. *Piaget's Theory of Intellectual Development: An Introduction.* Englewood Cliffs, N.J.: Prentice-Hall, 1981.

Gumperz, J. J. "Conversational Inferences and Classroom Learning." In J. Green and C. Wallat (eds.), *Ethnography and Language in Educational Settings.* Vol. 5. Norwood, N.J.: Ablex, 1981.

Holt, G. S. "Inversion in Black Communication." In T. Kochman (ed.), *Rappin' and Stylin' Out: Communication in Black America.* Chicago: University of Illinois Press, 1972.

Jensen, A. R. "How Much Can We Boost IQ and Scholastic Achievement?" *Harvard Educational Review,* 1969, *39* (1), 1–123.

Kochman, T. *Black and White Styles in Conflict.* Chicago: University of Chicago Press, 1982.

Kohn, M. L. "Social Class and Parent-Child Relationships: An Interpretation." In R. L. Coser (ed.), *Life Cycle and Achievement in America.* New York: Harper & Row, 1969.

Lave, J. "Cognitive Consequences of Traditional Apprenticeship in West Africa." Unpublished manuscript, 1976.

Leacock, E. B. *Teaching and Learning in City Schools.* New York: Basic Books, 1969.

LeVine, R. A. "Child Rearing as Cultural Adaptation." In P. H. Leiderman, S. R. Tulkin, and A. Rosenfeld (eds.), *Culture and Infancy: Variations in the Human Experience.* San Diego: Academic Press, 1974.

Ogbu, J. U. *Minority Education and Caste: The American System in Cross-Cultural Perspective.* San Diego: Academic Press, 1978.

Ogbu, J. U. *Cultural Inversion.* Unpublished manuscript, Department of Anthropology, University of California, Berkeley, 1981a.

Ogbu, J. U. "Origins of Human Competence: A Cultural-Ecological Perspective." *Child Development,* 1981b, *52* (1), 413–429.

Ogbu, J. U. "Cultural Discontinuities and Schooling." *Anthropology and Education Quarterly*, 1982, *13* (4), 290-307.
Ogbu, J. U. "A Cultural Ecology of Competence Among Inner-City Blacks." In M. B. Spencer, G. K. Brookins, and W. R. Allen (eds.), *Beginnings: The Social and Affective Development of Black Children*. Hillsdale, N.J.: Erlbaum, 1985.
Ogbu, J. U. "Cultural Influences on Plasticity in Human Development." In J. J. Gallagher and C. T. Ramey (eds.), *The Malleability of Children*. Baltimore: Brookes, 1987.
Ogbu, J. U. "The Individual in Collective Adaptation." In L. Weis (ed.), *Dropouts from Schools: Issues, Dilemmas, and Solutions*. Albany: State University of New York Press, in press.
Philips, S. U. "Participant Structure and Communicative Competence: Warm Springs Children in Community and Classrooms." In C. B. Cazden, V. P. John, and D. H. Hymes (eds.), *Functions of Language in the Classroom*. New York: Teachers College Press, 1972.
Philips, S. U. "Commentary: Access to Power and Maintenance of Ethnic Identity as Goals of Multicultural Education." *Anthropology and Education Quarterly*, 1976, *7* (4), special issue, 30-32.
Philips, S. U. *The Invisible Culture: Communication in Classroom and Community on the Warm Springs Indian Reservation*. New York: Longman, 1983.
Piaget, J. "Piaget's Theory." In P. H. Mussen (ed.), *Carmichael's Manual of Child Psychology*. Vol. 1. New York: Wiley, 1970.
Posner, J. "The Development of Mathematical Knowledge in Two West African Societies." *Child Development*, 1982, *53* (1), 200-208.
Price-Williams, D. R. "A Study Concerning Concepts of Conservation of Quantities Among Primitive Children." *Acta Psychologica* (Amsterdam), 1961, *18*, 293-305.
Price-Williams, D. R. "Abstract and Concrete Modes of Classification in a Primitive Society." *British Journal of Educational Psychology*, 1962, *32*, 50-61.
Price-Williams, D. R., Gordon, W., and Ramirez, M. "Skills and Conservation: A Study of Pottery-Making Children." *Developmental Psychology*, 1969, *1*, 769.
Ramirez, M., and Castenada, A. *Cultural Democracy, Bicognitive Development and Education*. San Diego: Academic Press, 1974.
Ruddle, K., and Chesterfield, R. *Education for Traditional Food Procurement in the Orinoco Delta*. Berkeley: University of California Press, 1977.
Saxe, G. B., and Posner, J. "The Development of Numerical Cognition: Cross-Cultural Perspectives." In H. P. Ginsburg (ed.), *The Development of Mathematical Thinking*. San Diego: Academic Press, 1983.
Scribner, S. "Recall of Classical Syllogisms: A Cross-Cultural Investigation of Error on Logical Problems." In R. J. Falmagne (ed.), *Reasoning: Representation, and Process*. Hillsdale, N.J.: Erlbaum, 1975.
Scribner, S. "Modes of Thinking and Ways of Speaking: Culture and Logic Reconsidered." Unpublished manuscript, Rockefeller University, 1976.
Seagrim, G. N., and Lendon, R. J. *Furnishing the Mind: A Comparative Study of Cognitive Development in Central Australian Aborigines*. San Diego: Academic Press, 1980.
Seeley, J. R., Sims, H. A., and Loosely, E. W. *Crestwood Heights: A Study of the Culture of Suburban Life*. New York: Basic Books, 1956.
Shade, B. J. "Afro-American Cognitive Style: A Variable in School Success." *Review of Educational Research*, 1982, *52* (2), 219-244.
Sharp, D., Cole, M., and Lave, C. "Education and Cognitive Development: The

Evidence from Experimental Research." *Monographs of the Society for Research in Child Development,* 1979, *44* (series 178), 1-2.

Shure, M. B., and Spivack, G. "Interpersonal Cognitive Problem-Solving and Primary Prevention: Programming for Preschool and Kindergarten Children." *Journal of Clinical Child Psychology,* 1979, *2,* 89-94.

Shure, M. B., and Spivack, G. "Interpersonal Problem-Solving as a Mediator of Behavioral Adjustment in Preschool and Kindergarten Children." *Journal of Applied Developmental Psychology,* 1980, *1,* 29-44.

Shure, M. B., Spivack, G., and Gordon, R. "Problem-Solving Thinking: A Preventive Mental Health Program for Preschool Children." *Reading World,* 1972, *11,* 259-273.

Shure, M. B., Spivack, G., and Jaeger, M. A. "Problem-Solving Thinking and Adjustment Among Disadvantaged Preschool Children." *Child Development,* 1971, *42,* 1791-1803.

Stevenson, H. "Influences of Schooling on Cognitive Development." In D. A. Wagner and H. W. Stevenson (eds.), *Cultural Perspectives on Child Development.* San Francisco: W. H. Freeman, 1982.

Vernon, P. E. *Intelligence and Cultural Environment.* London: Methuen, 1969.

White, B. L. *Origins of Human Competence: The Final Report of the Harvard Preschool Project.* Lexington, Mass.: Heath, 1979.

John U. Ogbu is professor of anthropology at the University of California at Berkeley and is a member of the Governing Council of the Society for Research in Child Development.

Participant observational research reveals that southern middle- and working-class Black parents differ in who they accept as primarily responsible for children's language learning. Educators must understand culturally different uses of language and aim to foster varieties of extended discourse.

Language Socialization

Shirley Brice-Heath

Since the 1960s, educators, employers, and the public media, as well as linguists and psychologists, have given considerable attention to the language of Black children and their families. Most of the publicity has focused on the differences in form between standard English and what has come to be called Black English vernacular (BEV). Linguists have demonstrated that Black English and its regional and social variants follow rules and are not random collections of errors or deviations from standard English (Labov, 1972). Moreover, linguistic studies have repeatedly pointed out that all Blacks do not speak BEV and, of those who do, most usually speak some standard English and use BEV only with some speakers, on some occasions, or for certain topics or recounted stories. As is the case with all types of English around the world (for example, Indian English or Nigerian English), Black English has regional and social varieties that allow the fine-tuning of language for style shifting and different communication needs (Baugh, 1983).

The research literature has concentrated on the forms of BEV. Far less frequently discussed have been the contexts for learning language that different types of Black communities and families provide for their children. In general, educators and clinicians have inferred the full range of language abilities of all children from the children's performance on standardized tests, in experimental situations, and in academic settings. Especially in the 1960s and early 1970s, such assessments generally reported low levels of early linguistic abilities in speaking, reading, and writing for Black children, especially among the poor or those attending inner-city schools (for a review of this literature, see Slaughter and Epps, 1987). Only in the late 1970s did researchers try to develop approaches that could tell them something about actual, rather than inferred, socialization environments of Black children in different types of communities.

This chapter begins with a brief discussion of both the research approaches and the model of socialization needed to consider the learning environments of Black homes and communities. It continues with a review of the current state of knowledge about the language socialization of Black middle- and working-class families within this model. The chapter closes with a discussion of implications for those who want to improve Black children's academic achievement.

Inside Families: How Does Learning Happen?

The premise that poverty and minority status produce a diminished home environment that does not stimulate academic achievement and high levels of aspiration has traditionally guided the research questions and methods of most educators, clinicians, and social scientists. Accepting a unilinear pattern of physiological and neurological development, researchers measured the progress of all children along a standard scale of maturation and assumed certain universal "normal" programs of socialization for all children, regardless of sociocultural background. Those who studied language acquisition focused primarily on the nature and order in which children acquire particular grammatical forms (such as tense markers or plurals), with the expectation that all children would fit generally into the same pattern of development and that all contexts of language learning would be similar. Differences would be demonstrated only in the language forms that appear in the language(s) children learn to speak. Thus, when studies characterized Black children as deficient in language development and their mothers as insufficiently supportive in verbal prompts, challenges, and evaluations of their children's performance, linguists and psychologists judged the home environments to be responsible for preventing children from following the normal pattern of language development.

Yet, also in the 1970s, social historians, anthropologists, and folklorists began to describe the extraordinarily rich verbal life of Black Americans found in rhymes, stories, songs, and interactions in churches, street life, and entertainment. African traditions, adaptive communicative behaviors formed during slavery, and strong extended family and religious supports were found to undergird numerous contemporary uses of language in Black communities (Folb, 1980; Levine, 1977; Smitherman, 1977; Whitten and Szwed, 1970). If the richness of jazz, rhyming, and folktales pervades these communities, how could these children be the victims of language poverty? Clearly, neither the questions researchers asked about home habits of reading and talking nor the experiments carried out in clinical settings reflected the kinds of language-learning environments Black families provided for their children.

Through improved statistical techniques, naturalistic studies of the immediate and larger contexts of family life, and greatly expanded areas of questioning to include more than those habits customarily believed central to socialization, some researchers began to link structural features with particular social processes in family life (Blau, 1981; Bronfenbrenner, 1979). Differences in the sources and ranges of language provided by the organizational ties of mothers, the spacing and number of children in a family, and the flexibility of interpretation and response in religious alliances helped predict the academic achievement of Black children. The sociologist Blau showed that, when Black mothers have nondenominational religious affiliations, maintain stability in the labor force over a number of years, and have a limited number of children, their children's academic scores are positively affected. The larger contexts of contact by family members, as well as the immediate home environment, help influence opportunities for language use and learning. Subsequent studies have shown that authoritative (firm but supportive) parents are those who find encouragement for the characteristics of persistence, assertive problem solving, and adaptability in their kin ties and voluntary affiliations (Spencer, Brookins, and Allen, 1985).

Yet, in spite of these studies, most of which did not focus on language, researchers still knew little about what goes on in the daily language life of Black children of different socioeconomic classes. Anthropologists who studied how children in distant societies learn to become members of their sociocultural group spent years living among these groups, learning their languages, and observing ways that adults orient the young to future roles as cultural members (see, for example, Mayer, 1970; Whiting and Whiting, 1963). Some of the ethnographies conducted inside and out of the United States were published as part of the Case Studies in Education and Culture series, edited by anthropologists Louise and George Spindler (see, for example, Peshkin, 1972; Rosenfeld, 1971; Ward, 1971). The model of socialization that dominated this work accepted the individual child as a recipient of transmitted knowledge and parents as the agents primarily responsible for transmission. Therefore these studies gave little attention to the socially interactive ways in which children create and negotiate the occasions, tasks, and extent of their learning, and the role of language in the socialization of children received almost no attention.

The influence of Soviet psychologist L. S. Vygotsky and of those scholars in the United States who helped to spread information about his work (for example, Michael Cole, Vera John-Steiner, and James Wertsch) led to new understandings of socialization, including the change from a transmission model to a dynamic view of the child as an actor negotiating transition and transformations (Rogoff and Wertsch, 1984; Vygotsky, 1962, 1978; Wertsch, 1981, 1985). Subsequent approaches to studying children's socialization have placed the child at the center of a network of potential modeling and teaching resources that change across time (Wentworth, 1980). This model sets aside the child as a passive but receptive learner and focuses instead on the child as an active learner helping to create the environment for acquiring skills, information, and affective response.

Moreover, this dynamic model acknowledges the continuous state of change and sources of change for the family and community that make it necessary for children to learn how to adapt through knowing when to apply, discard, reform, and supplement the facts and skills taught or modeled by others. For those anthropologists and linguists concerned with how children across societies learn language, this model of socialization acknowledges that when children learn language, they acquire more than the forms of grammar: They learn to make sense of the social world in which they live and how to adapt to its dynamic social interactions and role relations. In the reciprocal processes of social interaction that symbolic forms make possible, children develop a system of cognitive structures as interpretive frameworks and make a commitment to the common value system and sets of behavioral norms shared by their sociocultural group (Schieffelin and Ochs, 1986).

If children learned their language as they become socially acceptable members of particular sociocultural groups living in certain locations at particular times, then social scientists could study this socialization most intensively by becoming, to the extent possible, participant-observers in their sociocultural communities. Such studies could complement the research of those social scientists who use survey methods, interview techniques, clinical tests, or experiments and would serve as an especially valuable supplement of contextual information for tape recordings made at home by the parents or by means of automatic timing mechanisms (see Chapter Three). However, these methods of long-term fieldwork, acceptance as a participant-observer, and language fluency present special problems in the study of language socialization among Black American families. Relatively few Black anthropologists or linguists have chosen to focus their research on language and culture patterns of Black Americans. Barriers of racism and differences in social class must be overcome by Whites or non-American Blacks who undertake long-term fieldwork in Black neighborhoods, and in some places and during certain periods, these barriers have been insurmountable. All of the available studies of the contexts for language socialization among Black families have been done in the South or in northern urban communities of families who recently migrated from the South, and authors of these studies have been White women, traditionally allied in various ways with Black women and their children (Heath, 1983; Stack, 1975; Ward, 1971).

The Language Socialization of Black Children

Language socialization includes all the ways that the social interactions of children enable them to learn the forms and functions of their language, as well as the ways that those around them use language in order to facilitate children's sense of using language as a way to become a member of a particular sociocultural community (Schieffelin and Ochs, 1986). The ways individuals learn language in order to understand their relationships with family, kin, and friends are group-specific, and a particular group's members share values, behaviors, and beliefs as a result of the historical, economic, social, and religious factors that created the group's sense of identity. Thus, Black families in the nineteenth and twentieth centuries have developed different patterns of language socialization as a result of their relative degrees of access and entry into particular class structures, employment opportunities, and religious networks. It is therefore inappropriate and inaccurate to generalize to all Black families studies that report on only one segment of a group or only one community. The following findings are drawn from studies of southern families who were, during the period of research (late 1960s to late 1970s), undergoing the first decade of social desegregation and a period of relatively low unemployment in the region's textile mills (Heath, 1982a, 1982b, 1983, 1986a; Ward, 1971). Members of most families not only had experienced some years of association with rural life but also had lived for some period "up North."

Middle-class families either owned their own businesses or worked as professionals (ministers, teachers, dentists). The adults were graduates of southern Black colleges, many had spent some time in military service or living in northern cities, and all expected their children to attend college, become community leaders, and stay in the mainstream of American life. Their children's lives were filled with extracurricular activities, and parents and children alike belonged to numerous voluntary organizations, ranging from national sororities and fraternities to regional church fellowships.

Working-class families worked in local textile mills, as day laborers, or as domestics or traveled periodically to one of the region's large cities to find temporary work. Participation in church life depended on transportation; most families attended the "home" church in the rural areas in which their families had grown up. Many had not completed the eighth grade in school but had dropped out of school during their first pregnancy or to go to work to support their parents and younger brothers and sisters. They believed that a high school diploma would help ensure their young of jobs that were better than those they themselves held, and they wanted their children to do well in school.

Though the families of these two classes shared many ritualized uses of language, such as rhyming, telling local folktales, and raising hymns, they socialized their children to use language in quite different ways, and they used language differently in talking to and with their children. Middle-class men and women, many of whom had grown up in rural areas near the families of working-class children, used BEV on numerous occasions among themselves and with working-class Blacks. They knew how and when to joke, jest, threaten, and brag in verbal performances, and their children grew up seeing them do so. However, their children did not grow up playing with working-class children; their leisure hours were spent in activities with voluntary associations, sports, music lessons, and homework, all accomplished with their middle-class friends. Thus, their repertoire of verbal performances traditionally characterized as Black was considerably more narrow than that of their parents, and their performances tended to be modeled from figures in commercial entertainment or from local individual performers. Children of the middle-class families succeeded in school, and those who had particular difficulties in one or another content area received tutoring, special consultations, and alternative routes to fulfilling requirements. Their ways of using language, habits of reading and writing, and expectations of school's match of values with those at home helped them negotiate their own social and academic goals.

Children of the working-class families used BEV most of the time, switching to standard English for certain performances (such as going to the principal's office) as they matured or for giving the dialogue of speakers of standard English when telling a story. Their ways of answering questions, requesting clarification, using information from written materials, and negotiating what they wanted out of a situation differed markedly from those of their middle-class peers and those of their teachers.

Middle- and working-class families differed on five primary dimensions of language socialization. Fundamentally, the two groups approached their sense of responsibility and expectations of children in quite different ways as a result of their past and current work life, social relations, and affiliation with religious and group identification values.

Distribution of Critical Functions, Including Primary Language Source. Social scientists who have described modern, complex societies have tended to think of certain roles and functions as closely tied: Biological mothers are assumed to play primary nurturing roles; children have novice roles until certain societal institutions declare them responsible or ready for expert roles. Similarly, those who have studied language have assumed that mothers are the primary source of language input for children; the titles of literally hundreds of language acquisition studies have some term indicating mother-child interaction. Such studies assume that mothers' sense of role, availability, and preferred tasks will focus on nurturance and communication with their young children.

Middle-class Black mothers have tended to accept this role assignment for themselves or to take charge of hiring someone to take their place during certain hours of the day. However, in working-class Black families (and in many societies of the world), mothers are not the primary caregivers or source of language modeling for their children. Instead, communities immerse children in multiparty communication, and several members of the family and community may take on caregiving roles. When older children look after younger ones, some adults in the community "watch over" the caregiving and intervene only when something goes wrong. Under these arrangements, young children hear the talk of those close in age to them most directly and receive much talk from adults through their sibling caregivers (for example, "Tell that child to stop crying").

Type of Talk Addressed to Young Children and Expectations of Their Roles as Conversationalists. In the course of focusing on mother-child interactions in language learning, researchers have characterized the type of talk that mothers direct to their babies and toddlers as *baby talk* (Schachter, 1979; Snow and Ferguson, 1977). In general, these studies of middle-class mothers and children show that "motherese" is a simplified language, offered during nurturing routines and play and giving rise to certain verbal routines and games that emerge around the here and now of the immediate physical world. Through such interactions, children are to learn their role as conversationalists and their responsibility for answering questions addressed to them for which their questioners know the answer.

Middle-class families used these dyadic exchanges to structure the conceptual world of their children and to accommodate the world to their young (Ochs and Schieffelin, 1984). They focused children's attention on labels—the names of objects, events, and attributes—and they expected children to answer known questions to display the children's labeling abilities. Similarly, adults asked children to recount or retell the chronology of events the children had witnessed or taken part in (Heath, 1986a, 1986b).

Working-class Black families did not accommodate the world to their children; they expected the children to adapt to the situations offered by the world: "Children have to make their own way in this world," "come up," "have their own heads," and "take what the world gives out." The many speakers that surrounded young children as the children grew up did not simplify their talk for children or even feel the need to address the children directly, except on occasions of displays of affections. When caregivers asked questions of children, they did so to get an answer they did not know or to obtain information (Heath, 1982a). They expected children to do rather than say what the children knew: to imitate others' behaviors, recognize voices on the phone, and solve problems independent of adult help.

Uses of Oral and Written Information. Middle-class families belonged to regional and local organizations, received publications from these organizations, and belonged also to book clubs. They kept books as part of household decorations and used written materials in their daily work, religious life, and voluntary or leisure activities. They read and wrote as individuals, and they used writing to help them in their decision making (movie reviews, shopping ads, announcements of community activities). They took their children to the library, and they gave books and writing or art materials as gifts to children of all ages (Heath, 1982b).

Working-class families used telephone books, newspapers, and mail as sources of information and action (funeral announcements, advertisements). However, they usually depended on talk about these with community members to supplement the written information: Neighbors offered judgments on the merits of one store's canning supplies over another's, and front-porch get-togethers negotiated the meaning of school announcements and of changes in tenant reponsibilities. Children's lives centered on activities, and they rarely read or wrote except during times of playing school or doing homework. Finding either approval or space for individual pursuits in reading and writing was not easy. Working-class families acknowledged the importance of written materials for their church life, but they often depended on certain key individuals to keep records, prepare written materials, and report to others what they should know or do as a consequence of written rulings. The spoken word of another meant much more than a written message.

Expectations of Variants of Language to Be Learned. Middle-class parents used standard English, with various degrees of formality and regional dialect marking, in the bulk of their interactions with individuals in formal roles (postal workers, telephone operator, principal, professor). At home, they maintained informal standard English except when topic, ritual, audience, or situation called for BEV or some other variant of Black English. Between fraternity members, greetings were often Black, whereas conversations about local group activities and business transactions were in standard English. Among older Blacks, young adults, or adolescents, certain rituals of Black English signified alliance. Parents expected their children to learn to use the range of language variations appropriately, and they corrected their children when the children used BEV on Blacks who were family associates.

Working-class Black children heard BEV throughout most of the interactions of their daily lives. Standard English was performed for them frequently—on television and radio and in the stories they heard adults tell using the appropriate voices and dialects of actors. However, these occasions of standard English were not interactive; children were not required or expected to respond verbally to and with those who spoke standard English. To be sure, public encounters with grocery store clerks, postal workers, and the like might be in standard English, but children rarely heard anyone correct their dialect or explain why one or another expression should be used because it was good English. Thus, adults in working-class communities modeled a variety of functions of language for children, for example, jive talk, fussing, and sermons, in the framework of people of different ages, stations of life, and relative degrees of power communicating to accomplish certain goals.

Judgments of the Competence of Children. Middle-class families placed high value on their children learning to talk about what the children had done and were planning to do and on having the children "explain themselves." They tutored children in how to give directions, accurate comprehensible accounts of an activity (such as a ball game), and summaries of past accomplishments without boasting.

Working-class families, who often depend on children learning multiple roles at an early age, tended to stress learning by observation, apprenticing, and commitment to the necessity of the task. If no food was in the house, someone had to get food; if none of the dishes were clean, anyone could be responsible for clearing the sink. Tasks did not go to certain people only. Adults often scolded children for not "opening your eyes" or "looking out for your own self." Adults expressed the philosophy of "what's done is done" and did not ask children to recount for them either what the children had done or were currently doing.

However, given the appropriate time and audience, a child's poetic, clever, entertaining account of either the child's own experiences or those of another could receive high praise and strong rewards in interactional reinforcement. Interpersonal competence demonstrated by appropriate judgment of what an audience wanted to hear gained high marks, but children could gain this competence only through close observation of details of personal negotiation styles, a sense of how people felt, and an appropriate assessment of time, space, and audience.

In short, these five features and their dimensions of difference in content and approach for language socialization rest on a fundamental distinction. Middle-class families saw themselves as the primary agents of their children's upbringing. Working-class families depended on children's potential, and the situation of the children's life had considerable agentry. A willingness to express and act on the perceived intentions of others differed markedly between the two groups.

Educating and Preparing for Change

These different orientations to language socialization had strong implications for teaching. The middle-class parents saw themselves as their children's teachers and oriented their young to respond to the teaching of others who had the formally designated role of teachers. These parents expected adults to intervene in actions to verbalize step-by-step actions, ask children to answer known questions, recount what was already known, and elicit and reward accounts by children in which the children asserted themselves as primary actors. Working-class families, on the other hand, depended on displays of knowledge that were nonverbal as well as verbal, expected the young to engage in trial and error, and did not value verbal or abstract displays of knowledge. Written materials had to enter particular contexts of expectations of use to be valued.

During the 1970s, some educators pushed hard for schools to acknowledge the richness of ethnic and cultural diversity found in student populations. This recognition sometimes extended to folktales and songs of the history of Black Americans, but it rarely penetrated to an understanding of the different uses of language that children from various social classes and home situations might bring to school. The era of individualized instruction that prescribed the same scope and sequence of skills for each child to learn at the child's own pace set all children into a pre-scripted pattern of learning. Reading kits, individualized instruction in mathematics, and programmed English packages tested each student in a hierarchy of learning through which everyone was presumed to move in the same order and at approximately the same speed. Shortly after individualized instruction came the call for back to the basics and teacher accountability. Together these two forces further constricted the degree and kinds of language opportunities children had in classrooms. The learning of specific skills, labels, and forms of recounting became the primary focus as teachers tried to ensure the best possible results for their students on standardized tests, most of which asked only that students identify, search and find, fill in the blanks, and provide brief answers. Numerous studies indicate the restricted kinds of talk children can engage in during class time, their limited opportunities to write pieces longer than a paragraph, and the relatively small amount of time they can spend reading during school (Applebee, 1981; Cazden, 1986; Goodlad, 1984).

What is needed is a public recognition that schools, the institutions society has traditionally relied on to prepare youngsters in communicative abilities, are no longer accomplishing this task, most especially in the nation's inner cities (Heath and McLaughlin, 1987; Coleman and Hoffer, 1987). Society's institutions must socialize the young not merely through transmitting skills and information from elders but also through engaging children in a network of resources that prepare young people for the interactive transitions and transformations of adult life. For classrooms, this means becoming places that promote, extend, and build the forms and uses of as wide a range of language as possible. All children need more than labels and recounts to participate in future job settings; they must have opportunities to build accounts of past events—their own and those of others—describe activities in process, and verbally lay out events or plans for the future. The issue is not the overly simplistic one often proposed during the 1970s of bringing the different language uses of cultural groups into the classroom and teaching these as content. Instead, educators must foster varieties of extended discourse, ranging from giving explanations and telling accounts of events to assessing outcomes and preparing formal oral and written reports. These are increasingly called for by employers who want workers to collaborate, interpret, and communicate.

Currently, middle-class Black publications and spokespersons emphasize intensified middle-class approaches to remediating the problems they acknowledge for contemporary Black youth; they look to families and schools as prime resources (Black Family Summit, 1984). Black mass-media publications, such as *Ebony* and *Essence,* frequently carry articles on topics such as the love, care, and well-being of children; single-parent households; and responsible Black parenting. Many of these articles explicitly acknowledge that modern-day America offers few of the psychological and spiritual supports of traditional Black life. These publications urge Black parents to see themselves as primarily responsible for their children and to consider the need to limit family size, focus on quality time with their young, and become role models that will pass on their "best qualities" to their children (Hatcher, 1982, p. 128). However, the fundamental expectations of this view of the family as central support system reflect the norms of past decades of nuclear families in which working fathers and homemaking mothers provided sustenance, communicative partners, and academic support for school-age children. Such ideal families today make up only 7 percent of American households, and the realities of the quantity and quality of time that families give to supporting children for the broadest possible language socialization or achievement orientation differ greatly from those of past eras (Edelman, 1987).

To contend with the patterns of work, housing density, and poverty-perpetuating processes, especially in many of today's urban Black neighborhoods, educators, employers, and the public media must attend to extending the supportive network for today's youth beyond the family and school. Middle- and upper-income professionals, especially Black professionals, can take leadership in this recognition by considering alternative sources of support that traditionally have thrived in the working-class community and have nourished for many of them as individuals the attitudes of persistence, adaptability to change, and assertiveness that enabled them to rise in socioeconomic status. Furthermore, Black organizations, such as churches, fraternities and sororities, and, possibly replacements or rebuildings of the Black pride organizations of the 1960s, have a critical role to play in acknowledging and responding to the challenge of enabling today's youngsters to participate effectively in the youngsters' primary cultural environment and to move knowledgeably into the mainstream of American economic and social life. It is within these organizations and with the support they can provide to supplement families and schools that youngsters have the best chances of language learning as the key source of strategies for achievement and individual growth.

References

Applebee, A. *Writing in the Secondary School: English and the Content Areas.* Urbana, Ill.: National Council of Teachers of English, 1981.
Baugh, J. *Black Street Speech: Its History, Structure, and Survival.* Austin: University of Texas Press, 1983.
Black Family Summit. "Charge to Task Force on Developing and Mobilizing Resources for Supporting the Black Family." *The Crisis,* 1984, *91* (6), 262-302.
Blau, Z. S. *Black Children/White Children: Competence, Socialization, and Social Structure.* New York: Free Press, 1981.
Bronfenbrenner, U. *The Ecology of Human Development.* Cambridge, Mass.: Harvard University Press, 1979.
Cazden, C. "Classroom Discourse." In M. C. Wittrock (ed.), *Handbook of Research on Teaching.* New York: Macmillan, 1986.
Coleman, J. S., and Hoffer, T. *Public and Private High Schools: The Impact of Communities.* New York: Basic Books, 1987.
Edelman, M. W. *Families in Peril: An Agenda for Social Change.* Cambridge, Mass.: Harvard University Press, 1987.
Folb, E. A. *Runnin' Down Some Lines: The Language and Culture of Black Teenagers.* Cambridge, Mass.: Harvard University Press, 1980.
Goodlad, J. I. *A Place Called School: Prospects for the Future.* New York: McGraw-Hill, 1984.
Hatcher, C. W. "On Responsible Black Parenting." *Essence,* 1982, *13,* 128.
Heath, S. B. "Questioning at Home and at School: A Comparative Study." In G. Spindler (ed.), *Doing the Ethnography of Schooling: Educational Anthropology in Action.* New York: Holt, Rinehart & Winston, 1982a.
Heath, S. B. "What No Bedtime Story Means: Narrative Skills at Home and School." *Language in Society,* 1982b, *11* (2), 49-76.
Heath, S. B. *Ways with Words: Language, Life, and Work Communities and Classrooms.* Cambridge, England: Cambridge University Press, 1983.
Heath, S. B. "Separating 'Things of the Imagination' from Life: Learning to Read and Write." In W. Teale and E. Sulzby (eds.), *Emergent Literacy.* Norwood, N.J.: Ablex, 1986a.
Heath, S. B. "Sociocultural Contexts of Language Development." In *Beyond Language: Social and Cultural Factors in Schooling Language Minority Students.* Sacramento: California State Department of Education, 1986b.
Heath, S. B., and McLaughlin, M. W. "A Child Resource Policy: Moving Beyond Dependence on School and Family." *Phi Delta Kappan,* 1987, *68* (8), 576-580.
Labov, W. *Language in the Inner City.* Philadelphia: University of Pennsylvania Press, 1972.

Levine, L. W. *Black Culture and Black Consciousness: Afro-American Folk Thought from Slavery to Freedom.* New York: Oxford University Press, 1977.
Mayer, P. (ed.) *Socialization: The Approach from Social Anthropology.* London: Tavistock, 1970.
Ochs, E., and Schieffelin, B. B. "Language Acquisition and Socialization: Three Developmental Stories and Their Implications." In R. A. Shweder and R. A. LeVine (eds.), *Culture Theory: Essays on Mind, Self, and Emotion.* New York: Cambridge University Press, 1984.
Peshkin, A. *Kanuri Schoolchildren: Education and Social Mobilization in Nigeria.* New York: Holt, Rinehart & Winston, 1972.
Rogoff, B., and Wertsch, J. V. (eds.). *Children's Learning in the "Zone of Proximal Development."* New Directions for Child Development, no. 23. San Francisco: Jossey-Bass, 1984.
Rosenfeld, J. *Shut Those Thick Lips.* New York: Holt, Rinehart & Winston, 1971.
Schachter, F. *Everyday Mother Talk to Toddlers.* San Diego: Academic Press, 1979.
Schieffelin, B. B., and Ochs, E. "Language Socialization." *Annual Review of Anthropology,* 1986, *15,* 163–191.
Slaughter, D. T., and Epps, E. G. "The Home Environment and Academic Achievement of Black American Children and Youth: An Overview." *Journal of Negro Education,* 1987, *56* (1), 3–20.
Smitherman, G. *Talkin' and Testifyin': The Language of Black America.* Boston: Houghton Mifflin, 1977.
Snow, C. E., and Ferguson, C. A. (eds.). *Talking to Children: Language Input and Acquisition.* Cambridge, England: Cambridge University Press, 1977.
Spencer, M. B., Brookins, G. K., and Allen W. R. (eds.). *Beginnings: The Social and Affective Development of Black Children.* Hillsdale, N.J.: Erlbaum, 1985.
Stack, C. B. *All Our Kin: Strategies for Survival in a Black Community.* New York: Harper and Row, 1975.
Vygotsky, L. S. *Thought and Language* (E. Hanfmann and G. Vakar, eds. and trans.). Cambridge, Mass.: M.I.T. Press, 1962.
Vygotsky, L. S. *Mind in Society: The Development of Higher Psychological Processes* (M. Cole, F. John-Steiner, S. Scribner, and E. Souberman, eds. and trans.). Cambridge, Mass.: Harvard University Press, 1978.
Ward, M. C. *Them Children: A Study in Language Learning.* New York: Holt, Rinehart & Winston, 1971.
Wentworth, W. M. *Context and Understanding: An Inquiry into Socialization Theory.* New York: Elsevier Science, 1980.
Wertsch, J. V. (ed.). *The Concept of Activity in Soviet Psychology.* Armonk, N.Y.: Sharpe, 1981.
Wertsch, J. V. (ed.). *Culture, Communication, and Cognition: Vygotskian Perspectives.* Cambridge, England: Cambridge University Press, 1985.
Whiting, J., and Whiting, B. (eds.). *Six Cultures: Studies of Child Rearing.* New York: Wiley, 1963.
Whitten, N. E., Jr., and Szwed, J. F. (eds.). *Afro-American Anthropology: Contemporary Perspectives.* New York: Free Press, 1970.

Shirley Brice-Heath is professor of linguistics and English and, by courtesy, of anthropology and education at Stanford University. She is also a special fellow for research and development at the Stanford Humanities Center and a fellow at the Center for Advanced Study in the Behavioral Sciences.

Intensive naturalistic study of middle- and working-class northern Black and White kindergartners' requestive language functions was conducted in both family and school environments. Situation, nature of the dyadic interaction, and request type were important influences, thus amplifying and extending earlier, more sociological, formulations.

Patterns of Information Requests

William S. Hall, Elsa Bartlett, Alva T. Hughes

The research reported in this chapter concerns the process by which members of different racial and social-class groups use their language to request information in conversational discourse. Its purpose is to evaluate certain claims by sociologists, psychologists, and others about the effects of socialization on the acquisition and organization of this language function. Although a substantial literature exists on the requestive system, it has not attended to ethnic and social-class issues. The role of the situation has been investigated (Garvey and Bendebba, 1978; Wilson and Zimmerman, 1986), as has the illocutionary aspect of utterances (Ninio, 1986). The role of verbal interaction (Moerk, 1985; Tomasello, Farrar, and Dines, 1984), the cognitive system (Conti and Camras, 1984; Klee, 1985), learning (Erreich, 1984), and repetition (Neilson, Dockrell, and McKechie, 1983) in the requestive system have all been investigated.

The research reported in this chapter is motivated by practical as well as theoretical issues. Basic is the claim, inherent in the work of Bernstein

---

The research on which this chapter is based was supported by a grant from The Carnegie Corporation of New York to William S. Hall. Support for data analysis was provided by the Computer Center and the Graduate School Research Board of the University of Maryland, College Park.

and other sociologists (Bernstein, 1958; Brandis and Henderson, 1970), that members of different social classes and ethnic groups are socialized to use language to accomplish rather different purposes and that this results not simply in superficial stylistic variations but in important differences in the intellectual functions made available to different members of the different groups. The claim is based on the assumption that the process of socialization involves acquisition of a particular identity that consists of the various culturally sanctioned roles a person is expected to play (for example, child, grandchild, girlfriend, student) and that these roles, in turn, consist of sets of social actions appropriate to particular social contexts. Among these are the various actions that are accomplished through speech, such as requesting, promising, denying, and at a somewhat different level of organization, persuading, planning, narrating, and so forth (see Mehan, 1979; Cole, Dore, Hall, and Dowley, 1978; Hall and Nagy, 1986; Hall, Scholnick, and Hughes, 1987). The actions of a person will depend on the social roles to be acquired. This assumes that speech actions are not learned in isolation but in terms of some set of social relationships and situations. This suggests that what a child learns, initially at least, is not some general set of context-free speech acts (for example, how to request information) but rather particular acts to be performed by specific persons in particular contexts (for example, how to request information from Mommy when she is trying to feed the baby).

Language Socialization

Crucial to our argument is the assumption that language is organized at the level of social action and the claim that systematic differences exist not only in the functions that language serves but also in the actual vocabulary and syntax of the utterances themselves. Thus, systematic differences in function are claimed to result in utterances that actually highlight, through their vocabulary and syntax, different relations and orders of relevance. Members of different groups, depending on their roles, would thus have different opportunities to encode these relations and interpret such encodings, and these differences in access to such behaviors are likely to have important ramifications for both intellectual growth and schooling.

The argument for the effects of discourse on intellectual functioning can be made at two levels, depending on whether the emphasis is on inter- or intrapersonal mechanisms. Sociologists and other social scientists, focusing on the former, tend to emphasize the effects of communicative mismatch, particularly in cases in which a child must interact with others who do not share knowledge of the structure of the child's home discourse. The effects of such differences, which are often both subtle and far-reaching, can be particularly devastating in schools in which the teachers and other children come from different social classes and have quite different expectations about the organization of social actions. For important discussions and demonstrations of such efforts, see the work of Cazden, John, and Hymes (1972); Hall and Freedle (1975); Hall and Nagy (1986); Gearhart and Hall (1982); Mehan (1979); and Hall, Scholnick, and Hughes, (1987).

In the school, the social consequences of a teacher's attitude toward a given "nonstandard" dialect can be profound. For example, it can affect the teacher's initial judgment about the intelligence of children who use such a dialect, how they will fare as learners and be grouped for instruction, and how their contributions in class will be treated. This in turn affects the children's attitude about themselves as learners, their willingness to participate, and their expectations about results of their participation. The consequences of nonstandard speech with respect to a person's standing with peers may also be profound. It is often suggested that high status in peer and school settings requires opposing rules for using or not using language in various ways.

The effects of differences in the organization of requests for information and their responses are likely to be particularly important in school, as it is clear that the student's role in classroom instruction contexts consists, in large part, of interpreting and responding to the teacher's requests for information (see Mehan, 1979). For example, certain patterns of early language socialization perhaps also hamper children's ability to engage in instructional dialogue when they enter school—that is, the kind of communicative situation in which teacher and pupil engage in a question-and-answer routine in which the questioner has a specific answer in mind and the answerer's job is to guess what that answer is. The big difference between this type of interaction and the "normal" question-and-answer exchange is that the correctness of the answer is not necessarily judged on the truth value, but rather on its conformity to a strategy or plan for answering that the teacher has already constructed. In the context of this chapter, the question is, Does the communication environment provide an opportunity to engage in interactions that are similar to those of instructional dialogue? Here "similar" is used in the sense that the requirements of a correct answer are based on some ability to intuit the kind of answering strategy that the questioner has in mind rather than on truth value or some aesthetic organization of the speech act.

Perspectives from Cognitive and Developmental Psychology

Cognitive and developmental psychologists have focused on intrapersonal mechanisms, arguing for the social origins of many inner cognitive organizations. Vygotsky (1962, 1978) and others (see Wertsch, 1985a, 1985b) have claimed that the organization of problem-solving and reasoning behaviors in an adult depends, in large part, on a kind of planning or ordering of task behaviors that has its origins in language and that retains, even in its mature form, certain languagelike characteristics. Vygotsky uses the term *inner speech* to describe such planning and organizing, arguing that it amounts to an interiorized abbreviation of overt discourse. Given this framework, it is easy to see how the form of mature problem solving and reasoning can derive from the kind of discourse that surrounds problem-solving behaviors, for it is this discourse that will eventually be interiorized as the model for organizing these cognitive behaviors.

Exposure to different models of problem-solving behaviors is likely to result in different ways of conceptualizing a problem-solving task or, more profoundly, in different definitions of what might constitute an appropriate circumstance in which to engage in problem-solving behaviors. For example, patterns of language socialization that characterize some cultures or classes are often said to interfere with a child's ability to analyze and make analytical statements about certain kinds of behavior not always reflected on in everyday life. These include perceptual awareness (the ability to analyze a perceptual array into a set of geometrical or mathematical relationships) and behavioral awareness (the ability to analyze the emotions of a person or those of a fictional character). To understand how being a member of a given speech community might affect the ability to make this type of analysis, we must consider whether different cultures provide differential opportunities to engage in the kind of aforementioned metabehavioral analysis (Hall, Scholnick, and Hughes, 1987).

Arguments about the effects of patterns of language use on problem-solving and reasoning skills are not the only ones that can be made. Differences in language use must also affect public access to a person's ideas and consequent opportunities for elaboration. At a deeper level, different types of speech involve different opportunities to engage in certain basic cognitive processes. For example, the process of modification, in the case of adjectives or adverbs, or the process of subordination, the case of conjunctions, could easily be affected by different language use, particularly as these processes lead to different syntactic realizations and differences in vocabulary.

Differences in the way in which information is requested are probably especially important for cognitive development. To ask a question is to engage in structuring information into two parts: a part that is presupposed (or known) and a part that is problematic (or unknown). This suggests that the process of asking (and answering) questions might foster facility with the cognitive processes required to make such judgments and, at the same time, enlarge the domain over which such processes operate. Systematic lack of opportunity to construct such requests in certain social contexts and with respect to certain kinds of knowledge may seriously hamper intellectual growth.

Toward Specific Hypotheses

There are many reasons to expect systematic differences in the pattern of information requests found in the conversational interactions of family members from different social classes. Researchers such as Mitchell-Kernan and Ervin-Tripp (1977) and Hall, Nagy, and Linn (1984) have reported a variety of differences (including functional differences) in the language produced by lower- and middle-class children and adults from both Black and White ethnic groups in a number of different laboratory tasks, including describing pictures, participating in structured instructional interactions, and responding to interview schedules.

These results have led researchers to hypothesize a number of differences in everyday family conversational interactions that are correlated with differences in social status. Thus, for example, it has been proposed that lower-status families function in an environment that is relatively impoverished with respect to the exchange of verbal information (Hess and Shipman, 1965). Among other things, this suggests that lower-status families, in contrast to higher-status ones, will produce fewer requests for information in conversational discourse. At the same time, it has been suggested that, even within the existing information environment, children from lower-status groups will have fewer opportunities to participate in cross-generational family interactions: that information requesting will be dominated by adults.

Other researchers have proposed that the conversational interactions in lower-status families are likely to be relatively "noisy," making it more difficult for a new participant to enter a conversation and maintain new conversational topics. This suggests that information requests are more likely to receive no response and are more likely to be repeated in lower-status families.

Most important, many researchers have also hypothesized a serious mismatch between the conversational experiences of lower-status children at home and the verbal interactions required in school. Much of this theorizing has centered on children's experiences with "examination" questions. These questions, which tend to dominate instruction interactions, are somewhat different from other types of requests for information in that the information explicitly requested is already available to the questioner. Rather than requesting unknown information, these questions seem to function as requests for a display of the addressee's knowledge. The claim is that children from higher-status groups are much more likely than children from lower-status groups to have experienced these examination questions in everyday family conversational interaction and as a result are better prepared to cope with such questions in school. Reviews of these issues can be found in Hall and Guthrie (1981) and in Hall, Nagy, and Linn (1984).

Unfortunately, it has not been possible to test any of these hypotheses directly, as a suitable corpus of family conversation simply has not been available. The research presented here was designed to provide such a corpus and to assess the following hypotheses: (1) Members of various social groups will differ in the frequency with which questions are used to request information, in the type of information requested, in the extent to which various types of persons utter and respond to various types of requests, and in the extent to which various members succeed in obtaining responses, and (2) patterns of information requests in upper-status family conversations will more closely resemble the pattern encountered in school, particularly with respect to the pattern of "examination requests."

Information need not, of course, be obtained through overt question asking. In most situations, information can readily be requested nonverbally, through gestures and various noninterrogative utterances. Nonetheless, it seems reasonable to begin a study of information requesting in family discourse by focusing on overt question-asking behavior. We have already pointed out the importance of overt question asking and answering in school performance and have outlined arguments concerning its possibly crucial role in the development of many cognitive skills. Additionally, there are methodological reasons for focusing on questioning. In recent years, considerable progress has been made in specifying language use in conversational interaction. Schemes have been developed for describing a number of language functions, including a number of different types of information requests (see Dore, 1977). Fortunately, there is considerable agreement about criteria necessary for appropriate description. Identification of information requests requires analysis at the level of the speech act.

Method and Procedures

Speech act analysis involves a number of thorny problems, both practical and theoretical (see D'Andrade and Wish, 1985). For a start, it is not at all clear what evidence should be used in determining the function of a particular utterance: Should the investigators base their judgment on an assessment of the speaker's intentions or the listeners' interpretations of an utterance? In most cases, the two appear to coincide, but problems occur when they do not:

(1) *Mother:* Are your hands dirty, Leon?
   Child: Uh-huh.
   Mother: Well, dinner's ready now, stop fooling around, go wash them.

It is possible that the mother's first utterance was intended as a request for action (hand washing), but since it appeared in an interrogative form, Leon took the option of treating it as a request for information. That the mother may have intended her utterance to be interpreted as an action request is bolstered by the fact that she responds to Leon's utterance with an imperative, but the fact that Leon responded as if she had requested information makes the categorizing of this utterance difficult for the researcher: Whose point of view should be adopted?

Similar problems emerge in the following example:

(2) *Teacher:* Now I want you to listen very carefully. We're going to get ready to go downstairs. (*In a louder voice*) Is someone talking? Do I hear someone talking? (*Softer voice*) Now when I call your name I want you to . . .

Intuitively, the listener feels that the teacher's questions function as requests for action (stop talking), but it is no easy matter to describe how such a categorization is achieved.

The theoretical issues surrounding these problems have been explored at length by Grice (1975); Labov and Fanshel (1977); Dore, Gearhart, and Newman (1978); Ninio (1986); and others. They are extremely complex and could not be resolved in our research described here. It was necessary, though, to achieve some consistency in our data analysis, which meant that we needed to arrive at some reasonably coherent classification procedures.

One reasonable strategy was to design a system that classifies utterances primarily on the basis of the listener's response; we were interested in a description of conversation as a set of social facts and in the assumption that a conversational act becomes a social fact only if it secures uptake. Its characteristics as a social fact would then depend, to a considerable extent, on the kind of uptake (or response) that it secures (Goffman, 1974). In the case of information requests, then, the researcher might start with the notion that questions can be classified as requests for information if, in fact, they elicit or secure "informative" responses. How then can such responses be defined?

In part, the problem can be handled syntactically: Various interrogative forms have grammatically canonical responses (Carroll, 1986). For example, "when" questions are canonically responded to with temporal constituents, such as "today," "after the game," and so forth. Topic may play an even more important role in defining informative responses. For example, in the following text the mother appears to answer the child's request informatively even though her response is syntactically non-canonical, presumably because the two utterances share a common topic:

(3) *Child:* When am I going to get another cookie?
    Adult: You had four chocolate chips already. That's enough.

For a start, then, it might be said that it is the syntactic and topic relations between adjacent (nearly adjacent) utterances that serve to identify informative responses to requests. Sometimes, of course, requests do not appear to elicit a response. The teacher's questions in (2) provide one example; the first adult's question in (4) provides another:

(4) *First adult:* When you bringing the car around?
    Second adult: I told him never mind, we didn't need to get that TV fixed right away.
    Child: We ain't even going to be watching that program anyway.
    First adult: Uh-huh.

Intuitively, the questions in (2) and (4) seem to serve different functions: One is a request for action; the other, for information. The fact that a listener can perceive a difference indicates that the listener is able to make judgments about function on the basis of the requests themselves, independent of the responses. Theories about how persons do this involve important notions about the expectations and assumptions concerning requests that members of American culture bring to conversational interaction. These have been discussed by Labov and Fanshel (1977), Garvey and Bendebba (1978), Leech (1974), and others.

On the basis of the work of Labov and Fanshel (1977), we can say that both requests for action and information derive from a common set of expectations about requests in general. These common expectations may reflect a common origin: Both action and information requests may originate in a single, requestive communicative function that seems to emerge sometime during the child's first year (Bates, 1976; Bruner, 1975). These shared expectations or assumptions about the requested action (in the case of information requests, the providing of the requested information) include (1) both the action and the request are needed (that is, the listener would not provide the information unless asked); (2) the listener has the ability to perform the action (to supply the information), (3) the listener is either obliged or willing to perform the action, or (4) the speaker has sufficient status to have the right to tell the listener to perform the action.

Information requests differ from action requests in that the former involve an additional assumption about the current state of both the speaker's and the listener's knowledge. An utterance is interpreted as a request for information if the listener believes that the speaker does not already have the information on which the request focuses and if the listener also believes that the speaker thinks that the listener has the information.

An Investigative Example

The analytic scheme was designed to capture the aforementioned common set of expectations about requests. Procedures for the identification of information requests, then, acknowledged two kinds of information. When possible, positive identification depended on the presence of an informative response. When no such response could be identified, utterances were judged to be requests for action or information depending on whether they met the conditions specified in the foregoing assumptions or presuppositions. Information requests appear in several syntactic guises; although most are interrogatives, imperative and declarative forms exist as well.

Information requests can be further subdivided according to topic and type of information. Examination of our conversational data indicated that the topic of an inquiry involves one of three aspects of the ongoing social situation: the form of a particular utterance, the attitude of participants towards particular utterances, and the actual content of utterances. Requests about content were further divided into two categories: those concerning referential aspects of the discourse (persons, events, places, purposes, properties, locations, relationships, and so forth) and those concerning intended actions (information concerning permission to act and permissible choices). Referential questions were further categorized in terms of the type of information requested: In some cases, speakers seem to request the information itself, and, in other cases, speakers seem to request information about the state of a listener's knowledge with respect to a particular topic about which the speaker already appears to have knowledge (for example, examination questions). Additional information on the criteria used for differentiating among the requests can be obtained from William Hall.

The subjects were 39 preschool children four and one-half to five years old divided approximately equally according to race and socioeconomic status (SES) as follows: eleven professional-class Blacks, nine professional-class Whites, ten working-class Blacks, and nine working-class Whites. Socioeconomic status was determined through the use of income and education indexes from the scale developed by Warner, Meeker, and Eells (1949). The families resided in the New York City metropolitan area and were randomly chosen from a list of volunteers.

Recordings were obtained with lightweight equipment worn by the "target" child in each family. Conversations were recorded in each child's home and kindergarten over a two-day period in a series of ten predetermined social situations: (1) at home before kindergarten, (2) on the way to kindergarten, (3) arrival at kindergarten, (4) directed activity (lessons), (5) free play, (6) on the way home from kindergarten, (7) arrival at home, (8) before dinner, (9) dinner, and (10) before bed.

Target children wore vests with microphones sewn in; field-workers clipped microphones on their ties. Although adults and nontarget children in the study did not wear microphones, the two microphones used were, in general, sensitive enough to pick up all significant verbal interaction experienced by the children in the study. The children and their families were aware, of course, that they were being taped, but this caused little if any disruption of normal activities.

The target children wore their vests without protest; their movements were not restricted and they seemed quickly to forget about having the vests on. As for the rest of the family, they occasionally made references (although relatively few) to the tape recorder being on, but the conversations were natural. Anyone who reads the transcripts can sense that the families were not putting on an act for the tape recorder; they tended to ignore it almost completely. The use of wireless microphones also made it possible to include speech by the target children that might not have been recorded otherwise, for example, monologues spoken while the child was out of the hearing of any visible listener.

Two male field-workers took part in the data collection, a Black field-worker with the Black children and a White field-worker with the White children. In the collection of data, the field-workers tried to be as unobstrusive as possible. They rarely initiated conversations but, if spoken to, attempted to respond naturally. One of the field-workers' responsibilities was to provide a verbal description of the context; where the recording took place, where the subject was, who the interactants were, and what the interactants were doing—both verbal and nonverbal behavior. Furthermore, the descriptions of context often included what happened before and after, as well as simultaneously with, verbal interaction.

In the original transcripts, speakers were identified in terms of seventeen categories. These have been grouped into five speaker categories: target children, other children (brother(s), sister(s), male child, female child), adults (mother, father, grandmother, grandfather, other male adult, other female adult), experimenter, and others (unknown person or group, several persons speaking simultaneously, TV or radio).

Results

Information requests were coded in one dinner conversation and one teacher-directed activity in the kindergarten for each family. These situations were chosen as prototypical examples of adult-led conversations in the sample. For coding, each family conversation was divided into five equal segments on the basis of the total numbers of conversational turns. The first, middle, and last segments were analyzed; these constituted the family corpus. The school corpus consisted of all utterances in the directed-activity sample. Through this method, the quantity of conversation for different target children was relatively comparable.

Conversational Turns. Both corpora consisted of conversational turns. Analysis of the total of dinnertime turns indicated racial and social-class differences. Results of an analysis of variance indicated a race-x-SES interaction, with Black working-class families producing significantly less talk and Black professional families producing significantly more talk than their White counterparts. In contrast, the school groups seemed to be quite similar. Results of an analysis of variance showed no significant effects for race or social class.

When we examined the extent to which conversational turns were taken by different types of participants, a somewhat different pattern emerged. For each corpus, three participant categories were used: adult (in the home: parents, other relatives, family friends; in the school: teachers and school aides), child (in the home: target child, siblings, friends; in the school: target child, classmates), and research assistant (person responsible for collecting the data; different person for White and Black samples). The percentage of turns taken by the three types of participants differed substantially among the four groups. Results of an analysis of variance indicated a significant race-x-participant interaction. The research assistant accounted for a much greater percentage of turns in the Black working-class corpus than in the White corpus. In contrast, the school data showed no significant racial or social-class differences.

Frequency of Requests. First, we compared the number of information requests by participants in the home and school samples. We had hypothesized that participants in Black working-class homes would produce the fewest number of requests, that White working-class participants would produce fewer requests than the other professional subjects, and that the number of information requests in the various classrooms would be similar.

An analysis of variance performed on the total number of requests excluding those spoken by and addressed to the research assistants resulted in significant main effects for socioeconomic status ($F=6.25$; $df=1, 33$; $p=0.017$), race ($F=4.32$; $df=1, 33$; $p=0.045$), site ($F=28.39$; $df=1, 33$; $p=0.0001$), an SES-x-race interaction ($F=4.83$; $df=1, 33$; $p=0.035$), and an SES-x-site interaction ($F=4.98$; $df=1, 33$; $p=0.033$). As we expected, many more requests occurred in school (Ms school=43.85; Ms home=14.96). Additionally, Whites produced somewhat more requests than Blacks (Ms White=33.28; Ms Black=25.53). Counter to our expectations, more requests occurred in the inner-city than in the professional samples (*Ms* working class=35.34, *Ms* professional=23.47). These results are clarified by the SES-x-race interaction, which suggests that the working-class effect may be due primarily to the large number of requests in the White working-class sample.

These results are further clarified by the SES-x-site interaction, which indicated that differences seemed to occur primarily in the school data (*Ms* professional=31.06, *Ms* working class=56.64); in contrast, the average number of requests in the working-class (*Ms*=14.04) and professional homes (*Ms*=15.89) were quite similar.

The results suggest that the White and Black professional and Black working-class data are all quite similar in the frequency of requests, both at home and at school. Although the White working-class home data are similar to the data for these groups, the school corpus contains almost twice as many requests. These results run exactly counter to our predictions in two respects: We had predicted that situation would interact with social group to produce greater differences in the home than in the school (that is, we had predicted that the school requested environments would be quite similar), but, in fact, differences were larger in the school than in the home. We also had predicted that race would interact with socioeconomic status and site to produce the fewest requests in the Black working-class homes. The predicted three-way interaction did not approach significance (F=0.0158), but trends in the data do show that the working-class Blacks had the fewest number of requests.

Request Type. Of course, frequency differences by themselves are not the whole story or even the most interesting part of it. Of considerably greater importance are differences in the patterns of participation and request types. We had predicted that there would be significant differences in the pattern of participant roles in the home corpus, with professional-class families engaging in significantly more cross-generational questioning. That is, we expected that professional-class adults would engage in greater questioning of children and that middle-class children would engage in greater questioning of adults. At the same time, we expected to find no significant differences in the pattern of school participation: In all groups, we expected that school adults (teachers and teacher aides) would question children more frequently than children would question adults.

To test these hypotheses, we examined speaker-addressee request dyads. We used two speaker categories (child, adult) and three addressee categories (child, adult, no response). When data were organized according to dyad, analysis of variance revealed an effect for dyad (F=58.17; df 1, 175; p=0.00), interactions of race-x-dyad (F=3.95; df=5, 18; p=0.002), site-x-dyad (F=21.73; df=5, 175; p=0.00), site-x-SES-dyad (F=2.35; df=5, 175; p=0.034), and the expected main effects for race (F=12.32; df=1, 35; p=0.001) and site (F=4.06; df=1, 35; p=0.001).

As we had predicted, teacher-to-child participant pattern dominated the school data. It is of greater interest, however, to consider the interactions with race and SES.

Although frequency of within-generation (child to child, adult to adult) participant patterns are similar, there are racial differences in cross-generational requesting. Whites produced more than twice as many child-to-adult requests than Blacks did. The frequency of adult-to-child patterns is also higher for Whites but may reflect the increased number of requests in the White working-class school sample. This seems all the more likely because there was a site-x-SES-x-dyad interaction, which indicates a high amount of adult-to-child request dyads in the working-class corpus. Separate analyses of home and school data reinforced these findings. Analyses of home data showed the expected main effects for race and dyad, tempered by a race-x-dyad interaction.

Again, the main differences seemed to involve cross-generational requests in the White sample. White children produced more requests addressed to adults and adults produced somewhat more requests addressed to children than occurred with Blacks. Overall, White adults produced more requests than Black adults did (*Ms* White adult=11.91; *Ms* Black adult=6.04). Additionally, the requestive environment was somewhat noisier for White adults; twice as many White adult-generated requests received no response.

When analyzed separately, school data revealed a significant main effect for race and dyad as well as the expected SES-x-dyad interaction, indicating that working-class children receive almost twice as many adult-to-child information requests. Given the main effect for race (*Ms* White=14.21; *Ms* Black=9.28), it might be expected that a race-x-SES-x-dyad interaction in the White working-class data would account for more of the adult-to-child requests. Although this interaction was not significant, the trends in the data lend support to this interpretation.

Overall, then, dyad data pointed to racial differences in cross-generational requesting in the homes and to both racial and SES effects in the schools, amounting to a tendency for teachers in working-class White schools to make more information requests of children.

Analysis of information request types sheds more light on these patterns. We had predicted racial and social class differences in amount of referential information requested as well as differences in examination requests in the homes and no differences in the schools. Once again, our predictions were only partially supported. Analysis of variance revealed a main effect for race, site, dyad, and request type, as well as interactions of race-x-site-x-request type-x-dyad. As we predicted, there were more referential requests in the White homes, but, counter to our prediction, there were no effects for social class. When we examined dyad effects in the home data, we found that Whites produced more cross-generational requests, especially of the child-to-adult pattern. When we examined the school data, we found a similar pattern. White children were more likely to address information requests to teachers and teacher aides.

Discussion and Conclusion

The purpose of the research described in this chapter was to test hypotheses about group differences in the use of language to request information in conversational discourse. Various hypotheses have been advanced to test the possibility that ethnic and social-class differences exist in the use of various language functions and that such differences might affect children's behavior. Specifically, it has been hypothesized that children's language behavior might be affected in the cognitive, social, and educational areas (see Hall and Guthrie, 1981). We have not actually tested these hypotheses in the research presented here. Rather we have focused on the prior step of establishing variation in the use of a particular language function in racial and social-class groups. At the level of social class, we sought to test the hypothesis, especially advanced by Bernstein (1958, 1971, 1973), that the socialization of various social classes and ethnic groups directs them to use language in different ways from groups who cannot be so classified.

Using requests for information as the dependent measure, we found that indeed membership in an ethnic group, social class, and situation affected speakers' (child and adult) displays of this function. The difference, however, was not always in the expected direction. For example, members of the working class produced *more* requests. There were, of course, interactions emanating from these results. Most important, situation was found to be an important effect on the use of the requestive system. Our findings highlighting the role of the situation in discourse processing agree with the findings from other research, notably that of Cole, Dore, Hall, and Dowley (1978) and Bruner, (1975). These researchers emphasize aspects of the situation that go beyond temporality, as we defined situation, to encompass such items as topic, task, and speaker-addressee relations. Finally, our data support the variable of cross-generational responding. Ethnic group differences seem to exist in this regard.

All in all, the claim in the literature of group (ethnic and social class) variation in the use of the request language function is a complex one. Variation is not simply highly correlated with group membership; it also interacts with such important variables as situation, nature of the dyad, and request type. This finding contrasts sharply with sociologically oriented findings (see Bernstein, 1958, 1971, 1973; and Hess and Shipman, 1965).

Several other points should still be made. First, it is important to specify some of the questions that our research did not address. For one thing, we were not concerned with the process of question selection: How a given situation or linguistic context determines whether a question will be asked. Similarly, we were not concerned with the problems of how syntactic forms are selected. Nor were we concerned with the interesting and important issue of question content or vocabulary. For the most part, our concern was focused on frequency of information requests, irrespective of specific content, the identification of participant roles (who queries whom), and the extent to which queries elicit answers.

References

Bates, E. *Language and Context*. San Diego: Academic Press, 1976.
Bernstein, B. "Some Sociological Determinants of Perception: An Enquiry into Subcultural Differences." *British Journal of Sociology*, 1958, *9*, 159-174.
Bernstein, B. *Class, Codes, and Control. I: Theoretical Studies Toward a Sociology of Language*. Boston: Routledge & Kegan Paul, 1971.
Bernstein, B. (ed.). *Class, Codes, and Control. II: Applied Studies Toward a Sociology of Language*. Boston: Routledge & Kegan Paul, 1973.
Brandis, W., and Henderson, D. *Social Class, Language, and Communication*. Boston: Routledge & Kegan Paul, 1970.
Bruner, J. "The Ontogenesis of Speech Acts." *Journal of Child Language*, 1975, *2*, 1-19.
Carroll, D. W. *Psychology of Language*. Monterey, Calif.: Brooks/Cole, 1986.
Cazden, C. B., John, V. P., and Hymes, D. H. *Functions of Language in the Classroom*. New York: Teachers College Press, 1972.
Cole, M., Dore, J., Hall, W. S., and Dowley, G. "Situation and Task in Young Children's Talk." *Discourse Processes*, 1978, *1*, 91-117.
Conti, D. J., and Camras, L. A. "Children's Understanding of Conversational Principles." *Journal of Experimental Child Psychology*, 1984, *38*, 456-463.
D'Andrade, R. G., and Wish, M. "Speech Act Theory in Quantitative Research on Interpersonal Behavior." *Discourse Processes*, 1985, *8*, (2), 229-259.
Dore, J. "Oh Them Sheriff: A Pragmatic Analysis of Children's Responses to Questions." In C. Mitchell-Kerman and S. Ervin-Tripp (eds.), *Child Discourse*. San Diego: Academic Press, 1977.
Dore, J., Gearhart, M., and Newman, D. "The Structure of Nursery School Conversation." In K. Nelson (ed.), *Children's Language*. New York: Gardner Press, 1978.
Erreich, A. "Learning How to Ask: Patterns of Inversion in Yes-No and Wh-Questions." *Journal of Child Language*, 1984, *11*, 579-592.
Garvey, C., and Bendebba, M. "An Experimental Investigation of Contingent Query Sequences." *Discourse Processes*, 1978, *1*, 1-13.
Gearhart, M., and Hall, W. S. "Internal State Words: Cultural and Situational Variation in Vocabulary Usage." In K. M. Borman (ed.), *The Social Life of Children in a Changing Society*. Hillsdale, N.J.: Erlbaum, 1982.
Goffman, E. *Frame Analysis*. New York: Harper & Row, 1974.
Grice, H. P. "Logic and Conversation." In P. Cole and J. Morgan (eds.), *Syntax and Semantics. III: Speech Acts*. San Diego: Academic Press, 1975.
Hall, W. S., and Freedle, R. O. *Culture and Language*. New York: Halstead, 1975.
Hall, W. S., and Guthrie, L. F. "Cultural and Situational Variations in Language Function and Use." In J. Green and C. Wallat (eds.), *Ethnography and Language in Educational Settings*. Vol. 5. Norwood, N.J.: Ablex, 1981.
Hall, W. S., and Nagy, W. E. "Theoretical Issues in the Investigation of Words of Internal State." In I. Gopnik and M. Gopnik (eds.), *From Models to Modules*. Norwood, N.J.: Ablex, 1986.

Hall, W. S., Nagy, W. E., and Linn, R. *Spoken Words.* Hillsdale, N.J.: Erlbaum, 1984.

Hall, W. S., Scholnick, E. K., and Hughes, A. T. "Contextual Constraints on Usage of Cognitive Words." *Journal of Psycholinguistic Research,* 1987, *16* (4), 289-310.

Hess, R., and Shipman, V. "Early Experience and the Socialization of Cognitive Modes in Children." *Child Development,* 1965, *36,* 869-886.

Klee, T. "Role of Inversion in Children's Question Development." *Journal of Speech and Hearing Research,* 1985, *28,* 225-232.

Labov, W., and Fanshel, D. *Therapeutic Discourse.* San Diego: Academic Press, 1977.

Leech, G. *Semantics.* Middlesex, England: Pelican, 1974.

Mehan, H. *Learning Lessons.* Cambridge, Mass.: Harvard University Press, 1979.

Mitchell-Kernan, C., and Ervin-Tripp, S. *Child Discourse.* San Diego: Academic Press, 1977.

Moerk, E. L. "Analytic, Synthetic, Abstraction, and Word-Class Defining Aspects of Verbal Mother-Child Interactions." *Journal of Psycholinguistic Research,* 1985, *14,* 263-287.

Neilson, I., Dockrell, J., and McKechie, J. "Does Repetition of the Question Influence Children's Performance in Conservation Tasks?" *British Journal of Developmental Psychology,* 1983, *1,* 163-174.

Ninio, A. "The Illocutionary Aspect of Utterances." *Discourse Processes,* 1986, *9,* 127-147.

Scribner, S., and Cole, M. *The Psychology of Literacy.* Cambridge, Mass.: Harvard University Press, 1981.

Tomasello, M., Farrar, M. J., and Dines, J. "Children's Speech Revisions for a Familiar and Unfamiliar Adult." *Journal of Speech and Hearing Research,* 1984, *27,* 359-363.

Vygotsky, L. S. *Thought and Language.* (E. Hanfmann and G. Vakar, eds. and trans.). Cambridge, Mass.: M.I.T. Press, 1962.

Vygotsky, L. S. *Mind in Society: The Development of Higher Psychological Processes.* (M. Cole, F. John-Steiner, S. Scribner, and E. Souberman, eds. and trans.). Cambridge, Mass.: Harvard University Press, 1978.

Warner, W. L., Meeker, M., and Eells, K. *Social Class in America: A Manual of Procedure for the Measurement of Social Status.* Chicago: Science Research Associates, 1949.

Wertsch, J. V. (ed.). *Culture, Communication, and Cognition: Vygotskian Perspectives.* Cambridge, Mass.: Harvard University Press, 1985a.

Wertsch, J. V. *Vygotsky and the Social Formation of Mind.* Cambridge, Mass.: Harvard University Press, 1985b.

Wilson, T. P., and Zimmerman, D. H. "The Structure of Silence Between Turns in Two-Party Conversation." *Discourse Processes,* 1986, *9,* 375-390.

William S. Hall is professor of psychology at the University of Maryland, College Park, and is a fellow of the American Psychological Association.

Elsa Bartlett is research assistant professor in the Department of Neurology, School of Medicine, New York University.

Alva T. Hughes is assistant professor of psychology at Manhattanville College, Purchase, New York.

The process of identity formation among Black children is determined by cognitive maturation, current situational factors, and previous socialization influences, including the nature and quality of ego defenses. Recent research and theory demonstrate the independence of Black racial attitudes and Black self-concept from early childhood through the adolescent years.

Self-Concept Development

Margaret Beale Spencer

The body of research generally addressed under the label *self-concept* is still an important area in studies on Black children. However, the word self-concept is a misnomer not only for the material reviewed in this chapter but also for the large number of studies conducted in this area on minority children. Further, the term self-concept is an inappropriate label for the inferences or assumptions made from the large corpus of empirical findings on group identity (another large body of experimental studies).

The question might be asked, What does the title of this chapter communicate or what function does it serve? It must be concluded that much of the research on self-concept permits an unemotional exploration of race and its impact on the life course development of Black children without actually discussing racism and its etiology. This approach to the issue of race often encourages an assumption about the need to "aid" the victims with their problem as opposed to supporting a multilevel interactive analysis of a maturing individual within a complex ecosystem (that is, a multilevel environmental system) during a particular psychohistorical period.

With that qualification, if a question mark is placed behind the title,

---

The preparation of this chapter was supported by funding from the Spencer Foundation and the W. T. Grant Foundation.

the correct version would be "Self-Concept Development?" The altered title more appropriately represents the content of the text, which examines the nature of the questions asked about the development of the self for Black children during the previous forty years. That is, although the scientific literature has been assumed to represent self-concept findings and theorizing about Black children, questions about the validity of the assumption bear examination, given a closer scrutiny of the construct.

Traditional Assumptions About and Approaches to the Self-System

Self-concept actually refers to an individual's awareness of his or her own characteristics and attributes and the ways in which he or she is both like and unlike others (McCandless and Evans, 1973, p. 389). It is generally understood that this awareness reflects the initial self versus nonself differentiation that occurs during the first year of life—that is, the initial *me* and *not me* differentiating process. This initial me versus not me sorting process has been observed in the behavior of children during mirror play as an awareness of physical and facial characteristics. Over time, it finally evolves into an objective awareness about the self as talkative, strong, healthy, dirty, a girl, a boy, and so forth. Most important, these descriptive or objective labels about the self have implications for another dimension of the self-system—namely, self-esteem. For the most part, Black children have been studied in the latter manner (esteem) as opposed to the former (self-concept). For example, from general observations, studies of mirror play (self-concept) have not been conducted on Black children.

More specifically, the value that children or youth place on themselves and on their associated behaviors and attributes represents self-esteem. Undoubtedly, self-esteem and self-concept are intimately related. Value judgments about what children learn about themselves are frequently so interwoven that it is unlikely that they themselves separate fact from evaluation. In sum, self-esteem reflects how a child or a youth regards himself or herself across a wide spectrum of activities.

On the one hand, self-concept concerns the young child's image of himself or herself as an individual; self-esteem, on the other hand, represents evaluations of those images. Finally, identity suggests an integration with perceptions of future development, that is, an awareness of group membership and the expectations, privileges, restraints, and social responsibilities that accompany that membership (McCandless and Evans, 1973, p. 390). Accordingly, a young girl recognizes that possessing certain physical characteristics means being a female before she understands what females are expected or allowed to do. Similarly, a young child's awareness of skin color will occur before comprehension that this may designate the child as a Chicano, African-American, or Native American, for example, and that such groups face certain hardships in a society dominated by White Americans and by particular biases transmitted through institutional structures in place at every level of the ecosystem.

Identity Processes: Sex Role and Group (Racial) Referents

Identity formation—which is more global and interactive than usually assumed—should be viewed as a process through which children gain knowledge of such matters as their names, race, sex roles, social class, and the meanings these descriptions have for their lives. Most important, although young children may not understand the reasons that underlie these ascriptive meanings, these meanings evolve in the context of the specific culture to which a child belongs. To put it another way, young children may quickly learn that they and their families are not welcome in certain situations solely as a function of their race—that is, by being a Black person. However, it would be highly unlikely that children would understand why being Black should result in social discrimination. Thus, the child's progressively differentiated understanding of self suggests a dynamic, life-course formulation of an identity.

There are several salient influences. The process of identity formation is determined by cognitive maturation, current situational factors, and previous socialization influences, along with the nature and quality of ego defenses. The process is quite complex and not unlike, in fact, other aspects of ego functioning, such as sex role and moral developments.

The components of identity processes are not new or emergent themes. In one form or another, the issues represent longstanding concerns. Researchers' treatment of these issues relative to sex role identity (versus assumptions made about group identity) is instructive—that is, the literature on sex role identity has benefited from a long legacy of sophisticated analyses and rich theoretical interpretations, particularly for White, middle-income males. On the other hand, the quality of thinking and research products in the area of race-related identity concerns have not been as advantaged. In fact, a comparison of research on sex role identity versus research on race-related identity reveals that variations in the level of inferences drawn show significant patterned differences that have severely limited the quality and quantity of scholarship available to date for policy initiatives, cross-disciplinary academic training, and general dissemination of child development information to the public.

Variations in the research questions pursued and interpretations made have had transformational effects on the lives of children. Relative to teacher training, for example, incomplete models of human development and research (that is, an exclusion of research on Black children) suggest that, by the year 2030, the majority of children in public schools in the

United States will be minority youth who, at the current rate, will continue to have inadequately trained teachers who are generally unable to address the children's particular needs. Teachers are unable to educate children effectively if the youth themselves are not objectively represented in the teachers' training experiences. Teachers who lack specific knowledge about minority child development cannot be expected to obtain successes with minority children. In fact, teachers' understanding is often inhibited by the focus on models of deviance. Educational policies born of limited information can serve only a reactive function as opposed to the proactive task of maximizing the educability of an increasingly visible and majority segment of the public education consumership: Black youth.

The last fifty years of speculation and empirical studies of the self-system for minority children have lacked an implicit or explicit awareness of the basic tenets of self-system development noted. For the most part, the traditional, oft-cited, self-concept theorists who described Black self-concept were usually concerned with children's racial attitudes or reference group orientation. That is, although generally interested in Black self-concept, their research designs more often tested for racial group differences in children's reference group orientation; theorists usually assumed that a low or negative Black self-concept existed because of the assumed unbuffered effects of racism. Importantly, despite myriad methodological problems, conclusions on self-concept were most often obtained from empirical studies of racial attitudes. Accordingly, notions or assumptions about the functioning of self-concept over a life span for an entire group (for example, Black persons or African-Americans) were presumed supported by data from studies on racial attitude or reference group orientation conducted with young, cognitively (and appropriately) egocentric Black preschool children. The major, and generally consistent, finding obtained for this age group has been that both the color black and Black persons are devalued. The conclusion inferred was the presence of self-hatred and general personal disorganization.

Specifically, if Black children had been studied and included as something more than a sample of convenience or for demonstrating a priori assumptions of deviance, then the available literature would be decidedly different. Furthermore, if the group had been studied from a human development perspective, then the problem of inferring life course (adult, specifically) interpretations from child behavior might have occurred sooner. Inferences about Black male school performance (which, on the average, is impaired at most points during the period of mandatory school attendance) might have been explained differently if interpreted from a perspective that included the unique developmental tasks and psychological disequilibrium that accompany experiences and life course decisions made during this period of enhanced psychological vulnerability for all youth, independent of caste and social-class considerations.

Finally, if interpreters of research on Black youth had simultaneously made inferences that linked persistent sociocultural conditions at the various levels of the ecosystem to the mental health status of those individuals who perpetuate the undergirding social structural conditions of contemporary American life itself, then quite different value-based discussions, associated policy initiatives, and mental health concerns (along with responsive diagnostic classifications) would be apparent. Instead, only value-based questions about the family structures for the victims (of oppressed and institutionalized conditions) themselves continue to represent a national concern. The issue is relevant because the *Diagnostic and Statistical Manual of Mental Disorders* (DSM-III) (American Psychiatric Association, 1980) has been successful in the classification of all other aberrant behaviors except racist behaviors. The issue is not unimportant given the human toll and social stress exacted.

The presumptions and assumptions characteristic of minority-focused research efforts remained in place and unchallenged until research conducted in the early 1970s by minority scholars. It should be underscored that the traditional research efforts were successful in showing the unchanging quality and structural embeddedness of Eurocentricity in the fabric of American society as perceived by cognitively astute, young, egocentric, Black preschool children. These children were able to discern and identify tables, walls, relationships, dolls, trucks, and Eurocentric beliefs about the color connotations associated with black and white objects and specific racial biases concerning persons (Spencer and Horowitz, 1973).

Most important about this tradition of research is the observation that the analogous situation or an equally myopic approach did not occur to the same extent in the sex role literature for women. Although Gilligan (1982) would agree that psychological researchers have systematically and persistently misunderstood women, there are differences when the assumptions made about women are compared with assumptions made about Blacks. The misperceptions about women have not included working assumptions of psychopathology and deviance. The accumulated scholarship on the psychology of (White) women may have been slow and uneven in quality, but it had no body of opinion (except for Freudian notions, perhaps) that required dismantling or a reactive (versus proactive) response to an assumption of deviance: deficit, yes; psychopathology, no.

The issue is critical because an in-depth understanding of identity processes across the life course serves a central function for the manifestation and support of human competence along with more general personality organization. For members of a minority group, independent of developmental status, gender, and socioeconomic status, issues of competence and psychological health, although central to social policy themes, remain a conundrum. The absence of a legacy of rich scholarship on identity processes by majority-group behavioral scientists, combined with a referencing pattern that overlooks or ignores new directions of research by minority scholars in the area, continues to place Black families and children, for example, at risk. Although the research in this area has been extensive, too often the concepts and methods used have been redundant and limited.

However, there have been several reviews of the vast number of studies produced during the previous four decades (see Aboud, 1986; Aboud and Skerry, 1984; Banks, 1976; Brand, Ruiz, and Padilla, 1974; Cross, 1985, 1986; Porter and Washington, 1979). When the two decades of research that occurred before the 1965 Moynihan report on the Black family are reviewed, consistency of empirical themes and concomitant deviant-linked interpretations are evident. First, the data suggested that young, preschool Black children generally evaluated the color black and Black persons in a negative manner. A pattern of identification with a White figure or with Caucasian-type physiognomic attributes was observed. The concomitant interpretive trend was not only that Blacks generally show personality disorganization but also that the Black family and the Black community were ineffective or incapable of protecting Black children. Although there were no data to support the conclusions of pathological problems and ineffectiveness, the assumptive conclusions had an impact on school desegregation policy and proposals for implementation (see Powell, 1974). Interestingly, however, there was no parallel influence on the nature and quality of training for majority-group teachers of minority-group children. As desegregation policies were implemented, Black youth, more often than not, found themselves in majority-group schools that (informally or formally) implemented dual educational programs within the same buildings or within the same classrooms. (A good illustration of this would be the primary class pictures and club photographs in school yearbooks, particularly in the South. Most noticeable is the racial homogeneity of primary grade classrooms and extracurricular activities.) Evaluations of Black students and consequent achievement patterns are often based on teachers' assumptions or judgments about the students' attitudes and/or efforts; school or home self-esteem appears to be more predictive for White students (Spencer, 1985b).

During the same two decades before the Moynihan report, in those studies that did pursue comparisons of self-concept and self-esteem, findings did not show lower self-esteem for Black children; studies often showed that the self-esteem of Black children was equal to or greater than that of their White counterparts. Because comparisons of achievements by Blacks and Whites generally showed Blacks doing less well, these findings were interpreted as suggesting that Black youths have an unrealistically high self-esteem. Obviously, scientists' interpretations of findings and anecdotal observations are affected by training (Slaughter and McWorter, 1985).

In contrast, the two decades of research after the 1965 Moynihan report suggest many new possibilities and more serious attempts to translate the fit between the environment and the organism and the associated tensions into a more sophisticated, inclusive model of intrapsychic processes that are supported by data and direct assessments of the constructs. The redirections and alternative interpretations, although still infrequently cited by mainstream scholars, have influenced the thinking and energies of individuals committed to building more inclusive models of human development.

Accordingly, in reviewing the two decades of research and speculation about Black children's self-system that have occurred since the 1965 Moynihan report, several questions are explored: What is actually known and/or what remains a consistent misinterpretation or confusion in the literature? What have been some of the alternative conceptualizations or theoretical redirections required for determining real facts from unwarranted assumptions? What do we need to know or what remains as pressing concerns? What are the policy implications for these data?

Understanding Identity Development of Black Youth

After Moynihan's published report in 1965, several key studies were issued in the 1970s (for example, Porter, 1971; Rosenberg and Simmons, 1971). These included literature reviews (Banks, 1976; Nobles, 1973) and broader theoretical approaches (for example, Spencer, 1975, 1976) that suggested alternative interpretations of the pathology-based conclusions about the findings on personal and group identities.

As noted, until the decade of the 1970s, the consistent finding of Eurocentric racial attitudes among young Black children was interpreted as suggesting general psychopathology or self-rejection. Studies that assessed racial attitudes, racial preferences, and color connotations—aspects of the child's reference group orientation—were interpreted as suggesting that the child's self-esteem was negative or low. For the most part, personal identity variables were not measured directly. Although data were discussed in terms of these variables (for example, self-esteem, self-concept), studies continued to replicate the Clarks' methodology (Banks, 1976) and assessed only aspects of the child's reference group orientation or group identity. Reference group orientation variables would include, for example, race identification, race awareness, racial attitudes, and racial preferences.

Most of the new methods, conceptual formulations, and interpretations were contributed to by minority-group scholars (for example, Alejandro-Wright, 1985; Cross, 1985; Hare and Castenell, 1985; Semaj, 1985;

Spencer, 1985a). When assessed directly, Black children and youth were often found to have equal or higher self-esteem scores when compared with Whites. The most important aspect of these findings has been the observation that these new directions in research and theory, generally introduced by Black scholars, have been infrequently cited by child development researchers. Although published reports were becoming increasingly and routinely available, textbooks continued to be written during this period as though new research findings did not exist.

Another important contribution during the two decades after the 1965 Moynihan report was the development of research approaches that included the simultaneous assessment of both personal identity (self-esteem) and young children's reference group orientations; early contributions were made by independent and simultaneous research efforts (see McAdoo, 1973, 1977; Spencer, 1975, 1976, 1982a, 1984). Spencer's research in the mid 1970s and 1980s was an expansion and modification of earlier programmatic research (see Spencer, 1970; Spencer and Horowitz, 1973). An important finding from this redundant research effort was the demonstration of the early independence of personal identity from reference group orientation or group identity in preschool children. That is, young, cognitively egocentric children could feel good about the self (that is, personal identity) while also showing the traditional Eurocentric orientation toward the cultural group (Spencer, 1976).

Another finding from research conducted during this period was the early predictive relationship of race awareness to cognitive maturation and the relationship of race awareness to the Eurocentric group identity orientation of young children (Spencer, 1976, 1980, 1981, 1982b). Race awareness seemed to function in a manner analogous to sex identity— that is, this newer research indicated cognitive underpinnings for the differentiation of racial groups (such as the child's early differentiation for gender membership). In sum, race awareness was found to be correlated with the child's knowledge of racial stereotypes and to have cognitive predictors (Alejandro-Wright, 1985; Semaj, 1985; Spencer, 1976, 1982a, 1982b, 1985a). For the first time, research conducted during this period demonstrated that the child's production of Eurocentric values was linked to normal maturational processes consistent with specific, caste-related ecosystem experiences (that is, the child's cognitive development and exposure to racially biased imagery).

During the early to middle 1970s, research suggested that the ecosystem experiences of many children were infused with positive imagery of Whites along with negative stereotypes of minority groups but that these perceptions were malleable—they were amenable to traditional learning models and could be changed (Spencer, 1970; Spencer and Horowitz, 1973). A variety of studies that used bibliotherapy techniques, social reinforcers, and Black culture-oriented curricula in nonpublic preschools served two important purposes. The studies showed that Eurocentric attitudes reflected a particular type of learning and, consistent with learning theory models, were amenable to manipulation. Having a Eurocentric orientation was not evidence of personality disorganization; that assumption was not supported under direct empirical tests that included the assessment of both constructs. The subsequent paradigms were different from previous assumptions about personality disorganization, and they demonstrated the learned quality of Eurocentric values. Furthermore, unlike the assumption of passivity for Black parents' child-rearing efforts and practices, more recent studies by Black researchers have demonstrated variations in parenting strategies as a function of parental perceptions of improved conditions and hope (Spencer, 1983, in press; Bowman and Howard, 1985).

Research findings reported during the last ten years on the intervening role of Black parents (Bowman and Howard, 1985; Spencer, 1983, in press) suggest that a compensatory cultural emphasis by Black parents serves an important interventional function. These empirical findings are important and confirm earlier speculations by minority-group theorists, such as Edward Barnes, about the buffering roles of Black parenting strategies and the Black community for the rearing of healthy Black children (Barnes, 1972).

The integration of the literature concerning the myriad labels for constructs was significantly aided, beginning in the early 1970s, by work of a minority-group researcher (see Cross, 1985, 1986) who stressed the need to differentiate studies into those measuring personal identity versus others that measured reference group orientation. The ordering of the studies into personal identity, reference group orientation, or a combination of the two has served a clarifying and informative function for the literature.

Research implemented by minority-group researchers during the decade beginning in the mid 1970s was instrumental in proposing developmental variations in the relationship between findings on personal identity and reference group orientation. Influenced by Piagetian theorizing, these scholars introduced an integration of differentiating studies of personal identity and reference group orientation along with an articulation of developmental influences (see Alejandro-Wright, 1985; Semaj, 1985; Spencer, 1976, 1982a, 1985a).

Two independent programmatic research strategies conducted in both the North and the South (each included the direct assessment of sociocognitive developmental constructs) yielded consistent findings across studies (Spencer, 1976, 1982b, 1985a). First, older, less cognitively egocentered children, as expected, showed less Eurocentric reference group orientations. In fact, cross-sectional and longitudinal research has demonstrated that older, less egocentric, minority-group children show the most pronounced pattern of decreasing Eurocentric reference group orientation along with improved or better performance on cognitive measures (see Spencer, 1982a, 1982b). The issue of developmental variation in the pattern of reference group orientation is important because, up until the early 1970s and as still reported in most texts, the assumption has been that the response patterns of young, egocentric children characterize the performance patterns for the entire group, independent of developmental stage. That is, inferences about middle-childhood, adolescent, and adult cognitions were inferred from data generally obtained on the sample of convenience: young, Black (most often lower-income) preschool children.

More recent research has also pointed to the influences of differentiated perceptions, affectivity, and cognition for reference group orientation (see the section on identity in Spencer, Brookins, and Allen, 1985), again suggesting the complexity and developmental interactions with exposure to stereotypical imagery, intrapsychic processes, and behavioral outcomes, while also demonstrating the buffering influences of specific child-rearing value strategies: the parental implementation of a compensatory cultural emphasis. Many questions and policy concerns still remain, however.

Policy Considerations

As indicated previously, since the 1965 Moynihan report and its evaluation of Black parental efficacy and family viability, several new directions of research have emerged for interpreting personal and group identity findings for minority-status persons. Although much of this research continued to focus on the earlier years through middle childhood, little research (either cross-sectional or longitudinal) has examined the implications of early stereotypical thinking for adolescent conflicts. That is, it is clear that under the best of ecosystem supportive conditions, adolescence is a very difficult period. The crisis of arriving at a comfortable and positive identity is, at minimum, often difficult for youth. The quality and developmental course of these (identity) processes are dependent on and interact with self-system developments for Black Americans because of the facts of color and racism and unchanging and minimally challenged social structural conditions. The transformation of the related institutional behaviors and barriers into forms more difficult to identify objectively makes their impact no less salient in the lives of minority-group children and youth. According to Erikson (1959), identity processes involve both the reconsideration of earlier identifications and the anticipation of adult roles; thus, issues of sex, adult work-role decisions, and so forth would appear to be only exacerbated or worsened by uncertainties about reference group membership and assumed reflected appraisals of that membership.

It seems important to understand whether the crisis of adolescence is influenced by the early internalization of an Afro-centered reference group orientation arrived at proactively in a supportive family and/or school system versus a group identity reactively accrued as a consequence of biologically based cognitive maturation and/or ecosystem-based ego-threatening experiences. It might be asked, Would differences in the quality of behavioral adaptations be apparent for those youth who have experienced consistent positive beliefs about the group?

Similarly, what impact might an adolescent's reference group orientation have for young adulthood issues of intimacy? Are the adolescent drives mediated by a specific reference group orientation? The issue is important because it has implications for perceptions of marriageability, for the viability of marital relationships, and for the stability of family systems, communities, and an entire people.

Although there has been an emergent analysis of the role of the family as a buffer between ecosystem-level stereotypes and cultural socialization in the home, some data suggest that more competent appearing youth emerge from families who deliberately supply a compensatory cultural emphasis as part of their child-rearing efforts (Spencer, 1983). What supportive (cultural specific) socialization roles do other microsystems play— for example, the church, the school, and the peer group?

The previous research proposals and questions have important implications for family policy. Given the myriad competing demands on minority family systems (lower-income families, in particular), it would appear critical to understand exactly what supports or resources are available to aid the family's efforts to maximize the developmental outcomes of its young; furthermore, what specific cultural (parental) values and supports are most beneficial? Relative to effective parenting, the issues of identification, maximization, and utilization of supports are important because of the one finding consistently demonstrated from research over the last forty years: Conscious and unconscious practices that support racism remain firmly entrenched in the fabric of American life at all levels and apparently emerge early in life. In fact, relative to early childhood socialization experiences, Slaughter and Dombrowski (in press) raise important cultural concerns in their review of children's social and pretend play. In terms of a global, continuous cultural context, they note the importance of carefully designed studies of play as a context for exploring this etiology of dominant majority-group children's socialization into attitudes of superior privilege and the simultaneous accommodation and adaptation of children to multiple cultural referential sources. Their analysis raises issues of importance for the breadth and scope of required interventions.

The problem of racism remains unclassified by DSM-III or other routinely used mental health indexes although it continues to permeate social structures and to undermine the potential for maximal human development, academic outcomes, and life course achievements for American minorities of color. A more interactive examination of Black self-system determinants as a function of broader identity processes is an important scholarly initiative that has critical policy implications. However, to date, it has remained more popular to examine the effects of White racism on Blacks as opposed to also exploring policy that would effectively alter, buffer, or null the fact and impact of racism. It is, however, apparent that the appropriate policy concerns should be dualistic or two-sided. On the one hand, exploring familial, community, and societal supports that ensure the maximization of competence and positive adaptational strategies for all of society's young is important. On the other hand, addressed as a policy initiative, researching methods for eradicating the institutionalized character, transformational states, and undergirding supports of American racism as a mental health issue and problem for society generally appears to be an equally, if not more, fruitful place to start.

References

Aboud, F. E. "The Development of Ethnic Self-Identification." In J. S. Phinney and M. J. Rotheram (eds.), *Children's Ethnic Socialization.* Newbury Park, Calif.: Sage, 1986.

Aboud, F. E., and Skerry, S. A. "The Development of Ethnic Attitudes: A Review." *Journal of Cross-Cultural Psychology,* 1984, *15,* 3-34.

Alejandro-Wright, M. N. "The Child's Conception of Racial Classification: A Socio-Cognitive Developmental Model." In M. B. Spencer, G. K. Brookins, and W. R. Allen (eds.), *Beginnings: Social and Affective Development of Black Children.* Hillsdale, N.J.: Erlbaum, 1985.

American Psychiatric Association, Task Force on Nomenclature and Statistics. *Diagnostic and Statistical Manual of Mental Disorders.* (3rd ed.) Washington, D.C.: American Psychiatric Association, 1980.

Banks, W. C. "White Preference in Blacks: A Paradigm in Search of a Phenomenon." *Psychological Bulletin,* 1976, *83* (6), 1179-1186.

Barnes, E. "The Black Community as the Source of Positive Self-Concept for Black Children: A Theoretical Perspective." In R. Jones (ed.), *Black Psychology.* New York: Harper & Row, 1972.

Bowman, P., and Howard, C. "Race-Related Socialization, Motivation, and Academic Achievement: A Study of Black Youth in Three-Generation Families." *Journal of the American Academy of Child Psychiatry,* 1985, *24* (2), 134-141.

Brand, E. S., Ruiz, R. A., and Padilla, A. M. "Ethnic Identification and Preference: A Review." *Psychological Bulletin,* 1974, *81,* 860-890.

Cross, W. E., Jr. "Black Identity: Rediscovering the Distinction Between Personal Identity and Reference Group Orientation." In M. B. Spencer, G. K. Brookins, and W. R. Allen (eds.), *Beginnings: The Social and Affective Development of Black Children.* Hillsdale, N.J.: Erlbaum, 1985.

Cross, W. E., Jr. "A Two-Factor Theory of Black Identity: Development in Minority Children." In J. S. Phinney and M. J. Rotheram (eds.), *Children's Ethnic Socialization.* Newbury Park, Calif.: Sage, 1986.

Erikson, E. "Identity and the Life Cycle: Selected Papers." *Psychological Issues*, 1959, Monograph 1, entire issue.
Gilligan, C. *In a Different Voice.* Cambridge, Mass.: Harvard University Press, 1982.
Hare, B., and Castenell, L. "No Place to Run, No Place to Hide: Comparative Status and Future Prospects of Black Boys." In M. B. Spencer, G. K. Brookins, and W. R. Allen (eds.), *Beginnings: The Social and Affective Development of Black Children.* Hillsdale, N.J.: Erlbaum, 1985.
McAdoo, H. *An Assessment of Racial Attitudes and Self-Concepts in Urban Black Children.* Office of Child Development Publication, no. OCD-CD-282. Washington, D.C.: Office of Child Development, 1973.
McAdoo, H. "The Development of Self-Concept and Race Attitudes in Black Children: A Longitudinal Study." In W. E. Cross, Jr. (ed.), *The 3rd Conference on Empirical Research in Black Psychology.* Washington, D.C.: National Institute of Education, 1977.
McCandless, B. R., and Evans, E. D. *Children and Youth.* Hinsdale, Ill.: Dryden Press, 1973.
Moynihan, D. *The Negro Family: The Case for National Action.* Washington, D.C.: Office of Policy Planning and Research, U.S. Department of Labor, 1965.
Nobles, W. W. "Psychological Research and the Black Self-Concept: A Critical Review." *Journal of Social Issues*, 1973, 29 (1), 11-31.
Porter, J. *Black Child, White Child: The Development of Racial Attitudes.* Cambridge, Mass.: Harvard Univesity Press, 1971.
Porter, J., and Washington, R. "Black Identity and Self-Esteem: A Review of Studies of Black Self-Concept, 1968-1978." *Annual Review of Sociology*, 1979, 5, 53-74.
Powell, G. *Black Monday's Child.* East Norwalk, Conn.: Appleton-Century-Crofts, 1974.
Rosenberg, M., and Simmons, R. *Black and White Self-Esteem: The Urban School Child.* Washington, D.C.: American Sociological Association, 1971.
Semaj, L. T. "Afrikanity, Cognition, and Extended Self-Identity." In M. B. Spencer, G. K. Brookins, and W. R. Allen (eds.), *Beginnings: The Social and Affective Development of Black Children.* Hillsdale, N.J.: Erlbaum, 1985.
Slaughter, D. T., and Dombrowski, J. "Cultural Continuities and Discontinuities: Impact on Social and Pretend Play." In M. N. Block and A. Pellegrini (eds.), *The Ecological Context of Children's Play.* Norwood, N.J.: Ablex, in press.
Slaughter, D. T., and McWorter, G. A. "Social Origins and Early Features of the Scientific Study of Black American Families and Children." In M. B. Spencer, G. K. Brookins, and W. R. Allen (eds.), *Beginnings: The Social and Affective Development of Black Children.* Hillsdale, N.J.: Erlbaum, 1985.
Spencer, M. B. "The Effects of Systematic Social (Puppet) and Token Reinforcement on the Modification of Racial and Color-Concept Attitudes in Preschool-Aged Children." Master's thesis, University of Kansas, 1970.
Spencer, M. B. "Racial Attitude and Self-Concept Development in Black Children." Paper presented at the meeting of the American Orthopsychiatric Association, Washington, D.C.: March 21-25, 1975.
Spencer, M. B. "The Social-Cognitive and Personality Development of the Black Preschool Child: An Exploratory Study of Developmental Process." Doctoral dissertation, University of Chicago, 1976.
Spencer, M. B. "Race Dissonance Research on Black Children: Stable Life Course Phenomenon or Fluid Indicator of Intraindividual Plasticity and Unique Cohort Effect?" In J. L. McAdoo, H. P. McAdoo, and W. E. Cross, Jr. (eds.),

Proceedings of the 5th Conference on Empirical Research in Black Psychology. Washington, D.C.: National Institute of Mental Health, 1980.

Spencer, M. B. "Personal-Social Adjustment of Minority Group Children." Final report of Project No. 5-R01-PMS-MH-31106 funded by the National Institute of Mental Health, 1981.

Spencer, M. B. "Personal and Group Identity of Black Children: An Alternative Synthesis." *Genetic Psychology Monographs,* 1982a, *103,* 59-84.

Spencer, M. B. "Preschool Children's Social Cognition and Cultural Cognition: A Cognitive Developmental Interpretation of Race Dissonance Findings." *Journal of Psychology,* 1982b, *112,* 275-286.

Spencer, M. B. "Children's Cultural Values and Parental Child-Rearing Strategies." *Developmental Review,* 1983, *3,* 351-370.

Spencer, M. B. "Black Children's Race Awareness, Racial Attitudes, and Self-Concept: A Reinterpretation." *Journal of Child Psychology and Psychiatry,* 1984, *25,* 433-441.

Spencer, M. B. "Cultural Cognition and Social Cognition as Identity Factors in Black Children's Personal-Social Growth." In M. B. Spencer, G. K. Brookins, and W. R. Allen (eds.), *Beginnings: The Social and Affective Development of Black Children.* Hillsdale, N.J.: Erlbaum, 1985a.

Spencer, M. B. "Racial Variations in Achievement Prediction: The School as a Conduit for Macrostructural Cultural Tension." In H. P. McAdoo and J. L. McAdoo (eds.), *Black Children: Social, Educational, and Parental Environments.* Newbury Park, Calif.: Sage, 1985b.

Spencer, M. B. "Parental Value Transmission: Implications for Black Child Development." In L. Burton, H. Cheatham, and J. Stewart (eds.), *Black Families: Contemporary Issues and Concerns.* Newbury Park, Calif.: Sage, in press.

Spencer, M. B., Brookins, G. K., and Allen, W. R. (eds.). *Beginnings: The Social and Affective Development of Black Children.* Hillsdale, N.J.: Erlbaum, 1985.

Spencer, M. B., and Horowitz, F. D. "Effects of Systematic and Token Reinforcement on the Modification of Racial and Color-Concept Attitudes in Black and White Preschool Children." *Developmental Psychology,* 1973, *9* (2), 246-254.

Margaret Beale Spencer is associate professor in the Division of Educational Studies at Emory University and an associate clinical professor of community medicine at Morehouse School of Medicine. She is currently a member of the Child Care Panel of the National Research Council of the National Academy of Sciences and a member of the Board of Directors of the National Black Child Development Institute.

Part 2.

*Studying Black Children:
Impact on Research
and Social Policy*

Since the 1960s, the study of African-American children has beneficially instigated or facilitated reformulation of research paradigms in developmental psychology, especially those paradigms addressing cognition, language, and cultural ecology.

The Study of African-American Children's Development: Contributions to Reformulating Developmental Paradigms

Dalton Miller-Jones

In this chapter I argue that contemporary concepts and methods of investigation in developmental psychology owe a significant debt to the study of African-American children. The thesis presented here is based on the premise that psychological constructs prevalent during the 1950s and early 1960s encountered serious challenges when applied to African-American children. The purpose of this chapter is to specify those challenges and to describe how they significantly affected the direction developmental theory and research was to take over the succeeding two decades.

To illustrate the contributions made by the study of African-American children to developmental psychology, I focus on the study of cognition and cognitive development. First, I establish what concepts and methods constituted the subdiscipline during the 1950s. Second, I specify what gave rise to changes in developmental concepts and methods in the 1960s. Third, I establish that there is more continuity between concepts and methods used today and issues raised during, rather than before, the 1960s.

By most accounts, the study of development experienced a period of rapid expansion and critical change from the 1950s through the 1970s. How did the study of African-Americans contribute to the reformulation of developmental psychology over this period? It is argued that (1) increased funding, both federal and private, on which the expanding developmental research enterprise depended, was made available largely in response to demands for social reform and restitution for past injustices on the part of African-Americans and other participants in the civil rights movement; (2) this unprecedented support acknowledged the legitimacy of a social science knowledge base in helping to form public policy, and also directed the course of future research by specifying the kinds of information and psychological understanding research needed to address; and (3) the emergence of more process-oriented models of cognition (both structural Piagetian and functional/contextual); a formal view of language as a social communicative process (sociolinguistics); multivariate research models; new approaches to assessment and more constrained interpretation of existing measures; and contextual accounts of competence, both in cross-cultural and subcultural research and in redefining environmental influences in terms of social ecology, can be traced, in part, to the inadequacies of prevailing paradigms most dramatically revealed in their applications to the study of children of African descent.

A Brief History

Throughout its history, developmental psychology has been influenced by social movements and societal pressures. In their discussion of changes in developmental paradigms, Bronfenbrenner, Kessel, Kessen, and White (1986) identify three periods of growth in developmental psychology: the child study movement (1900), the child development movement (1920-1930s), and the developmental psychology of the 1960s. According to these authors, each period is indebted to major changes in American social policy and initiatives at the federal level (see Bronfenbrenner, Kessel, Kessen, and White, 1986, pp. 1220-1223).

Wertsch and Youniss (1987) provide another sociohistorical account of the formulation of issues in developmental psychology, again pointing to the early twentieth century child-saving movement as the origin of the discipline. The child savers included Protestant and Catholic ministers, middle-class women, and professional educators who, as child advocates, sought to restrict child labor, to require school attendance, to introduce public health codes, and to establish custody based on children's best interest. Wertsch and Youniss conclude, "Exactly how the dynamics at religious and political levels entered the discipline or affected its orientations we cannot say" (p. 22). Missing from these historical acco[unt is] any explicit recognition of the impact of African-Americans on t[he disci]pline of psychology. Perhaps a careful examination of the social po[litical] contexts associated with more recent changes in the discipline can shed light on such dynamics.

In 1954 (*Brown* v. *Board of Education*, see Clark, 1963, pp. 158-159), the U.S. Supreme Court ruled:

> We must consider public education in the light of its . . . present place in American life. . . . Today it is a principal instrument in awakening the child to cultural values, in preparing him for later professional training, and in helping him to adjust normally to his environment. . . . We come then to the question presented: Does segregation of children in public schools solely on the basis of race, even though the physical facilities and other "tangible" factors may be equal, deprive children of the minority group of equal educational opportunities? We believe it does. . . . To separate them from others of similar age and qualifications solely because of their race generates a feeling of inferiority as to their status in the community that may affect their hearts and minds in a way unlikely ever to be undone. . . . Whatever may have been the extent of psychological knowledge at the time of *Plessy* v. *Ferguson*, this finding is amply supported by modern authority. Any language in *Plessy* v. *Ferguson* contrary to this finding is rejected. . . . We conclude that in the field of public education the doctrine of "separate but equal" has no place. Separate educational facilities are inherently unequal. Therefore, we hold that the plaintiffs and others similarly situated for whom actions have been brought are by reason of the segregation complained of, deprived of the equal protection of the laws guaranteed by the Fourteenth Amendment.

Two aspects of this ruling are important for the argument made here. First, in reaching this decision, the court relied significantly on testimony from "modern authority," that is, the social sciences (Clark, 1950; see Clark, 1963; where the text of the May 17, 1954, Supreme Court opinions appears in Appendix 2 and the text of the appellant's briefs on the effects of segregation and the consequences of desegregation appears in Appendix 3). Thus, a precedent was set for and a significant contribution made to establishing what is now a rapidly expanding subfield of legislative psychology. Second, in admitting both the importance of equal educational opportunity and its denial to "Negro" Americans, the stage was set for the massive Great Society-War on Poverty effort of the Johnson administration a decade later. The core propostion at the heart of these efforts was that social science knowledge, especially of development, had established a causal link between socialization practices in lower-class (disadvantaged, culturally deprived) homes and childrens' poor average academic performance in an astonishing number of areas. In addition to funding myriad direct intervention programs (for example, Head Start and later Follow-Through; see Chapter Six in this volume), funding was also provided for basic research. Combined with federal initiatives supporting educational innovation in science and mathematics (in response to losing the first round of the space race to the Soviet's launch of Sputnik), these two efforts represented a massive investment of federal monies and ushered in an unprecedented era of research on educational practices. The contention made here is that it was partly on the shoulders of African-American children and their families that major research programs in universities across the country were built.

The Cognitive Revolution

The two dominant paradigms operating in psychology in the 1950s were based on behaviorist (social learning) and psychoanalytic theories. However, in the late 1950s "research on human language, learning, and problem solving began to address the influences of complex internal processes (Bruner, Goodnow, and Austin, 1956; Chomsky, 1957; Miller, 1956; Newell, Shaw, and Simon, 1958) . . . [and] signaled the end of the behaviorist hegemony in North America" (Case, 1985, p. 39). This shift from the predominance of behaviorism to a focus on cognitive models and a related emphasis on processes (competence) underlying the products of task performance set the stage for the attention given to Piaget's theory of intellectual development that was to follow.

Piaget's reign over cognitive development has now begun to wane as certain aspects of the theory dealing with the invarient progression of stages and discontinuities in development resulting from the qualitative reorganization of structures of knowledge have been challenged by research (Laboratory of Comparative Human Cognition, 1982, 1983). Kuhn, (1983) observes: "in North America in the early 1980s, we find the field of developmental psychology in a transitional period in its own development. Compelled to characterize the major dimensions of this transition in a sentence or two, one would probably cite on the theoretical front the growing disillusionment with Piaget and the increasing utilization of information-processing models in work on cognitive development. On the methodological front, one might cite a decreasing confidence in laboratory studies and increasing concern for how the academic discipline should relate to real-world decisions of policy and practice" (p. 81).

There has been, I think, a bold break with the traditional view of reasoning as disembodied abstraction. In this view, literal propositions can be objectively determined as either true or false, and rational thought consists of the manipulation of symbols that get their meaning through correspondence with the world, objectively construed (Lakoff, 1987). Consequently, if a person does not share the conventional correspondences, the person does not fit the traditional model of logical thinking. Recent proposals offer a more inclusive conception of how humans make sense of experience (Neisser, 1985) or construct categories as a form of mental representation based on Rosch's (1975) theory of prototypes and basic-level categories, and provide for more imaginative mechanisms (for example, metaphor, imagery, and metonymy).

These challenges to linear information-processing models, and to the computer as a metaphor for human thinking, have their bases in efforts to account for rational thought as a function of the organism's experiences in everyday environments. The challenges support the position that all people, as is the case with generative universalists' views of language, have the same basic capacities to organize experience along conceptual dimensions. The dimensions themselves are dependent on context and experience such that in some areas similar conceptual systems will emerge (for example, Gould, 1980; Berlin, Breedlove, and Raven, 1974), whereas others will differ. Cognitive models have thus moved from conditions of absolute truth or falsity (that is, either they conform to a single view of correspondence to representations of reality or not) to one that includes gradiance and probabilistic qualities of concepts (Lakoff, 1987).

What role did the study of African-American children play in these historical changes in the field? Both behaviorist (social learning and verbal mediation theory) and psychoanalytic interpretative systems gave rise to the characterization of ethnically based poverty experiences as ones of the psychosocial and sensory deprivation. Ultimately, these views gave way to criticism and resulted in significant changes both in the notions of environmental influences and in the conception of specific processes in cognition and language.

In 1966, the U.S. Department of Health, Education, and Welfare commissioned four task forces to examine the enormous research literature on psychosocial deprivation and educational achievements of the disadvantaged (U.S. Department of Health, Education, and Welfare, 1968). In sections of the resultant volume, the contributions made to developmental psychology by the study of African-American children are apparent. Two aspects of the document make it clear that considerable soul searching was provoked when established paradigms in psychology were applied to African-American children. First, in introducing each section of the report, the Perspectives on Human Deprivation Task Force found it necessary to examine the basic assumptions and the principal conceptual features of prevailing theories of social, personality, learning, and cognitive development before presenting research data on deprived populations. For example, the authors acknowledge that the deprivation metaphor "has been a less than satisfactory guide to both conceptual and empirical efforts" (p. 2), and the concept was severely criticized when it was applied to environmental variation in psychologically defined variables. It is observed that deprivation-deficit models derived much of their initial force from work on maternal and sensory deprivation. The connotation was that to be disadvantaged "involves some kind of lack or insufficient exposure to abstractions in communication patterns" (p. 2). However, the authors state that (1) "norms or criteria for sufficiency are neither available nor established . . . we simply have no understanding of threshold values below which insufficiency can be defined" (p. 2). (2) "Conditions of disadvantage can often be characterized . . . by the *excess* of certain kinds of stimulation or environmental attributes" (p. 2). (3) "The deprivation metaphor is, to some extent, logically misleading in that it suggests that the explanation of the phenomena of disadvantage lies in what is absent rather than in what is present" (p. 3).

Second, although the report provides a useful compendium of information and is of historical significance, at least one reading of the document suggests a clear message: Existing knowledge and psychological theory and research methods are inadequate for understanding development in ethnically and socioeconomically diverse populations. This can be seen, for example, in the following areas of research, listed as priorities for the future: (1) more specific and precise definition of disadvantaged populations (present ones confound ethnicity, social class, and various conditions of disability) and research that examines variability both within and between groups; (2) research that uses more diverse social contexts, for example, naturalistic research in both classrooms and out-of-school settings; (3) systematic testing of Piagetian theory; (4) research on symbolic operations, particularly the forms of representation subserving categorization and classification; and (5) research on language development, including nonstandard English. Clearly, subsequent research, with not only African-American but also Anglo-American children, reflects this list of priorities and signals a substantial change in the direction developmental psychology was to take.

Reconceptualization of Intelligence. Difficulties encountered when attempting to interpret the performance of culturally distinct children on a wide variety of cognitive tasks led to important reassessments of the validity of the metrics themselves as well as their underlying constructs. In particular, attempts to assess African-American children's intellectual functioning most directly influenced the emergence of the competence-performance distinction (borrowed from psycholinguistic research) in areas of cognitive functioning and a radical reconceptualization of cognitive ability and intelligence.

Behind the infusion of massive public and private funds to solve the educational equity problem lay test scores pointing to the glaring disparity in academic achievement between African- and European-Americans.

Such performance data were initially taken at face value and gave rise to the early deficit-deficiency models (either genetic or environmental) to account for these differences. First, Cole and Bruner (1971) and later, in much more detail, Ginsburg (1972) exposed the problem of taking such products of performance as valid measures of underlying capacity or competence (see below). Although this distinction has broad-based applications and has subsequently been used in a wide variety of areas, its interpretive usefulness was first and most dramatically revealed in the area of assessing cognitive competence among diverse cultural groups.

The introduction of Piaget's (1970) theory provides an excellent example of how cognitive abilities were reconceptualized during this period. There were undoubtedly many reasons for Piaget's rapid ascendancy to a position of dominance in developmental psychology; among them was the theory's emphasis on cognitive processes (assimilation, accommodation, and equilibration) that prevail across wide areas of specific content. It is more than coincidence that these developments occurred during the critical debate over the appropriate assessment of cognitive abilities among ethnically distinct children. It might be asked, What was wrong with existing formulations of cognitive functioning that led to the ready acceptance of Piaget's ideas?

Measures of cognition prevailing in the 1950s relied heavily on factual knowledge and verbal ability, even when purporting to measure concepts. In an early departure from such views, Ginsburg (1972) argued that Piaget's genetic epistemology provided a better basis for understanding poor children's cognitive abilities. Ginsburg (1972) provided a careful review of research on poor children, mostly African-Americans, conducted during the late 1950s and 1960s. Two consistent generalizations emerged from this review. First, there are profound methodological problems with the research (for example, social class and ethnicity confounds) that make the findings and conclusions ambiguous, and there is a lack of clarity regarding precisely what standardized tests of achievement and ability measure.

Second, there is a strong recommendation for adopting the Piagetian framework as a conception of cognitive functioning and the clinical-interview method as a way of investigating cognitive competencies in culturally different groups. For example, instead of a perspective that considers infants of poor parents as cognitively deficient, Piaget's developmental view, stressing universally shared stages of cognitive development, is offered as a better conceptualization. Piaget's (1952) first stage of cognitive development stressed sensorimotor functioning. Ginsburg described research by Golden and Birns (1968) and by Wachs, Uzgiris and Hunt (1971) that investigated three areas of sensorimotor development (the object concept, ends-means behavior, and behaviors for dealing with objects). Wachs, Uzgiris, and Hunt found significant social class differences on means-end performances at all ages tested except fifteen months. However, in two areas, object concept and behavior in relation to objects, there were no essential differences between the poor and the middle-class samples. Ginsburg (1972, pp. 14-16) concluded that, with certain obvious exceptions such as organic impairment, all children, whether poor or middle class, share the same basic cognitive organization: "My conclusion, . . . the *developmental view*, is that in many fundamental ways poor children's cognition is quite similar to that of middle-class children . . . regardless of culture or upbringing. At the same time, there do exist social-class differences in cognition. Yet the differences are relatively superficial, and one must not make the mistake of calling them deficiencies or considering them analogous to mental retardation. . . . Poor children live in a unique environment. They hear a distinct dialect; they must solve problems that middle-class children cannot even imagine; they suffer special kinds of oppression, . . . These are all distinctive conditions with which the poor . . . must cope and for which they develop special accommodations, unique ways of behaving and thinking." My point is that, without the crisis of educational failure and controversy over veridical assessment of cognitive functioning among African-Americans, it is doubtful that Piaget would have been so warmly and widely embraced by American scholars.

There are two basic issues for the student of development here: first, the concept of intelligence itself and its measurement and second, the possible underlying mechanisms leading to particular levels of performance among individuals and groups of individuals.

The African-American contribution here has been one of challenging the constructs' lack of definition and forcing the consideration of multiple kinds of intelligences. For example, Meacham (1983, p. 122), observes: "The validity of the construct of intelligence . . . has been increasingly questioned (Samelson, 1975), especially as this construct has been applied in the evaluation of women and minorities . . . [and] . . . Riegel (1973) titled his introduction to a symposium on intelligence 'an epitaph for a paradigm,' expressing the view that is was necessary to construct new, alternative conceptions of intelligence that were more appropriate for these and other groups in a changing society. . . . [The] main criticism [of what Riegel calls the traditional accumulation model of intelligence] is that [the model] neglects uncertainties, doubts, and questions, and the role of social transactions in the construction of knowledge."

The issue is brought sharply into focus by Lesser, Fifer, and Clark (1965) who, in arguing against a conceptualization of intelligence as a single, general trait, show differential patterning in mental abilities among children from different social and ethnic groups. In a follow-up of this work, Stodolsky and Lesser (1967, p. 555) report that "the types of achievement and intelligence tests which are most often used can have only limited value in describing the cognitive functioning of children. . . . [looking at the scores on psychometric tests reveals little about] the ways the students arrived at a conclusion." Contemporary emphasis on processes underlying performance (Sternberg, 1985) and on multiple domains of competence, for example, language, mathematics, spatial representation, bodily movement, and personal relationships (Gardner, 1983), derive in part from the demands placed on the conceptualization and measurement of intellectual abilities necessitated by the study of African-American children.

There has always been a tension between formulations of intelligence that stress an innately given general "g" ability (Jensen, 1969) and those that view intelligence as a multifactor construct (Neisser, 1986). Two types of nativist arguments need to be distinguished: those that are psychometrically derived (such as heritability quotients), based on instruments purported to measure cognitive ability, and those that focus on inherent biological dispositions to form concepts, classify, and categorize, derived from developmental theory (Gelman and Baillargeon, 1983; Carey, 1985; Keil, 1981, 1986).

Psychometrically based nativist arguments posit traitlike capacities that determine the forms or qualities of thinking (such as Jensen's Level I associative and Level II conceptual abilities). Essential to this claim was the demonstration that such putative abilities distributed themselves differentially across groups with unique gene pools. Test performances of African-Americans constituted the central data for this renewed nature or nurture debate. Research over the ensuing two decades challenged this formulation. First, critical examination of the test instruments themselves revealed a lack of consensus in defining intelligence and its constituent underlying processes, and task analyses of items indicated that several interrelated skills are typically involved and that "no test of cognitive activity yields pure measures of any of the processes that psychologists designate as *the* process under consideration" (Laboratory of Comparative Human Cognition, 1982, p. 655).

Second, it has been argued that the construct of intelligence as represented in a single "g" or general factor is a statistical artifact of factor analytic procedures (Gould, 1981). Claims that quantitative differences in scores reflect qualitatively different intellectual processes have not been substantiated. Examination of specific children's performance has shown that although they may give associate-level responses on some items, they demonstrate conceptual abilities on others (Miller-Jones, in press). Furthermore, Boyce (1983) analyzed several large intelligence test data sets and identified those subtests and items that yield the largest differences between Blacks and Whites. If the psychometrically based nativist position were correct, then items involving abstract reasoning should have shown higher percentages of Anglo-Americans passing them. In fact there were no differences between Blacks and Whites on abstract-reasoning items. Instead, Boyce found the qualities of intelligence test items that did differentiate the populations included how the items were worded, the factual contents, and the reliance on visualization.

The African-American contribution was one of forcing and supporting a more formal articulation of the interactional processes underlying development, or how nature and nurture work together to produce adaptively fit organisms. This can be seen in the increasing attention to interactional explanations in behavioral genetic analyses characteristic of twin and adoption studies and in neonativist formulations positing biological constraints on cognitive representations (Carey, 1985; Keil, 1981). The contribution is also reflected in the shift from perceiving children as either having or not having a particular ability to one that views all children as having the same basic cognitive capacities. Children may differ, however, in how their repertoires of competencies are organized. In this conceptualization, experiences in particular cultural ecologies lead to different cognitive organizations and determine which cognitive processes will be accessed in a particular task or test environment.

Cross-Cultural Research. The late 1960s and the 1970s witnessed a burgeoning interest in and attention to cross-cultural research (Laboratory of Comparative Human Cognition, 1983). What stimulated this renewed interest in cross-cultural psychology and what has happened to these endeavors?

There is clear evidence that the increasing interest in cross-cultural research was motivated by the seemingly intractable problems of understanding development under conditions of poverty in the United States and that the methods and interpretative heuristics employed in the research have contributed significantly to developmental psychology. For example, in the preface to his book on Puluwat navigation, Thomas Gladwin (1970, pp. i–ii) writes:

> The book's beginnings and central purpose derive from the experiences of poor people in the United States. . . . [They] tend to do badly in school. They are also inclined to achieve low scores on intelligence tests. . . . Educators have . . . been handicapped in their efforts to remedy these intellectual deficits by a lack of clear understanding of how the quality of thinking differs between people who are poor and those not-so-poor. Tests can . . . pinpoint quantitative differences, but the results of testing educationally nonachieving poor people are far more ambiguous when it comes to isolating the specific *qualities* in thinking. . . . The failure thus far to identify clearly the distinctive characteristics of the thinking styles which develop under conditions of poverty has led to an impasse of tragic proportions. Schools keep penalizing children for the poverty into which they have unwillingly been born, while one remedial scheme after another

disappoints its sponsors by imparting only trifling or temporary benefits. A new approach is needed. This book is the chronicle of one effort to open such a new avenue of inquiry.

Research in non-western cultures was motivated by several concerns: Were some processing abilities universal, or did they vary as a function of culture? If universals are found, are they the result of some invariant feature of culture biologically determined? When variation is observed, what do people know that is culturally given and how, that is, through what processes, do they come to know it? The less frequently mentioned potential contribution is that cross-cultural research can serve as a test of the validity of psychological constructs used.

Cross-cultural research has had several significant consequences for developmental psychology. First, it has been discovered once again that the means or methods of describing cultural environments and psychological ecologies are sorely lacking. Second, when experimental research is carefully designed, and steps are taken to ensure task saliency, stimulus familiarity, and equivalency, and that questions are asked in ways appropriate to the particular culture, the major finding is that people share the same basic abilities. Third, how these processing abilities are organized and deployed varies between and within cultures according to specific features of the history of an individual's activities related to the task at hand (Laboratory of Comparative Human Cognition, 1983). This has led to the emergence of contextualist theories, for example, cultural practice theory (Scribner and Cole, 1981; Laboratory of Comparative Human Cognition, 1982), and the generation of symbolic and meaning-systems conceptualizations of culture in cognitive anthropology (see Shweder and LeVine, 1984). Thus, what began as an enterprise to understand cultural determinants of African-American performances on cognitive tasks has produced significant progress in methodology and in our conceptualization of cognition.

Language: A Social Communicative Device. Perhaps no other single area reflects the sweeping changes the field experienced during the 1950s through the 1970s better than language development. The perspectives on language and language development prior to 1957 are well represented by McCarthy's work (1954) in which language was viewed as "the amazingly rapid acquisition of an extremely complex system of symbolic *habits* by young children" (p. 492). In presenting an impressive and carefully detailed review of theory and research, McCarthy portrayed the study of language acquisition as proceeding in a quantitative fashion, involving normative count studies of overt speech. For example, infants' prelinguistic utterances (number and onset of vowels and consonants), the role of limitation, average age for first words, the growth of vocabulary, and changes in the grammatical complexity of sentence structure (for example, use of compound, complex, or subordinated phrases and use of modifiers) were reported. The primary psychological mechanisms thought to underlie language acquisition were conditioning (reinforcement) and imitation, although there was also a concern expressed for a focus on meaning, which leads the linguist "directly to the field of psychology, for he finds that meaning must be explained in terms of the situation in which the word is used" (p. 493).

However, in 1957, Chomsky introduced the distinction between articulated speech and the underlying phonological, syntactic, and semantic knowledge needed to produce it. Although Chomsky's generative-transformational grammar model of language, like Piaget's theory of cognitive development, has been challenged (in particular, the innate basis for a language acquisition device, and the difficulty of adequately specifying syntactic structures by using a minimal set of rules), the model has revolutionized the way language processes are conceptualized.

The central contributions made to the study of language by research on African-American children are in the areas of psycholinguistics and sociolinguistics. Research based on prevailing theories of language had labeled the African-American child as language incompetent in several dimensions. Whorf's (1956) linguistic relativity argument suggested, in its strong form, that the language of a culture constrains or determines thought. This argument was reflected in studies showing that (ostensibly lower class) African-American children were language delayed—producing shorter, more fragmented utterances (for example, Hess and Shipman, 1965); failing on verbal achievement and reasoning measures; and lacking in verbally based symbolic representational abilities necessary for abstract categorization—and essentially nonverbal (Bereiter and Englemann, 1966). Fundamental to Chomsky's generative-transformational view of language was the proposition that all human languages share the same basic properties—that is, they are abstract rule-governed systems and thus have equipotential for logical thinking. Although no case can be made that African-American children influenced Chomsky's formulation, it is important to recognize that research findings on Black nonstandard English and cross-cultural studies of language acquisition constituted significant, supportive verifications of his ideas.

Labov (1969, 1972) has been straightforward about the contribution of African-American culture to linguistic theory. He intended to influence the way linguists thought about language, namely to make the study of human language more inclusive of its social-communicative properties. In his view, the power of such an approach was to be most dramatically demonstrated by research revealing both the commonly shared underlying competence structure of Black nonstandard English and its unique sociolinguistic features (for example, dialogic and narrative competence). Labov, along with others (for example, Baratz, 1969), using the generative grammar perspective, found the African-American child fully competent as a linguistic entity. More than that, Labov went on to argue forcefully that the errors made in misunderstanding the language competence of inner-city minority children were due to a flawed and narrow conceptualization of language, which, in his view, is most essentially a social communicative device. Thus, the research on African-American children contributed significantly to establishing the field of sociolinguistics. Here, as in other areas, long-standing traditions share this claim (for example, McCarthy, 1954), but it was the empirical support for this position from the study of Black children that facilitated its movement to the forefront of the field.

Reconceptualization of the Cognitive Environment

During the period from the 1950s through the 1960s, there was little psychological attention to specific features of African-American culture as a determining variable (Tulkin, 1972). Instead, the experiences of African-Americans fell under the rubric of cultural deprivation–disadvantaged and were considered to be summated by socioeconomic-status variables, the approach by which the discipline primarily dealt, and still deals, with subpopulation variation. A number of other conceptualization problems still exist. Frequently, deprivation terminology may refer to all Blacks, and ethnicity and social class are regularly confounded variables in research with African-Americans. Often it goes unrecognized in regard to African-Americans that culture, as a set of adaptive processes operating independently of and interacting with social class, may play a significant role in determining socialization patterns and developmental outcomes.

Tulkin (1972) urged researchers to distinguish between status variables (class, race, and so forth) and process variables, which reflect the actual experiences of children that contribute to cognitive growth. He reported research that used process variables descriptive of interactions between parent and child (for example, parental press for academic achievement and language development). These studies obtained correlations of 0.76 to 0.80 between these process variables and IQ measures, which are substantially higher than the correlations of 0.40 to 0.50 typically reported between socioeconomic status and measures of intelligence and school achievement.

Today, there has been a major reconceptualization of environmental domains and influences as ecological contexts for human development. Instead of a theoretically loose collection of unconnected variables (for example, social class or socioeconomic status, ethnicity or race, family structure and so forth), the environment is seen as a series of interdependent interacting systems, at least in theory if not in journalistic practices. Related to this change is the utilization of multivariate designs and more powerful statistical procedures (for example, stochastic and structural equation models) in lieu of designs that stress linear influences of single variables and simple interaction effects. Progress in this domain resulted from the demands for more qualitative and descriptive research, especially concerning African-Americans, that would incorporate more variables and thus better represent the complexity of human functioning.

The Task Force on Human Deprivation (U.S. Department of Health, Education, and Welfare, 1968) explicitly states the failures of existing conceptions of environmental influences on development:

> What is needed to replace the explanatory contribution of the deprivation term is the refined and careful study of variation, variation in those attributes which are characteristic of the present in the environments to disadvantaged populations or statuses, and variations in their outcomes. . . . It becomes clear that a major—perhaps the fundamentally critical—obstacle to analytic understanding [of conditions of disadvantage] is the lack of a systematic theory of the psychosocial environment . . . an articulated *explanatory* account of behavior and development ultimately requires a proximal level of environmental analysis. No amount of degree of correlation between such distal variables as social class, economic status, minority group membership, . . . [and] behavioral attributes . . . can serve as substitute. . . . [Such correlations should be viewed as probabilistic indicators, and] lower-class life or minority group status should be seen . . . to be elliptical designations for bundles of proximal environmental attributes [pp. 3–5].

It is clear, from the preceding quote and in the Task Force recommendations for research, that subsequent expansion in the use of multivariable designs and more complex, ecologically valid and interactional system approaches in development research stem in large part from the challenges posed by the study of African-American children. McLoyd and Randolph (1985), in summarizing research on African-American children for the period from 1936 through 1980, reported that the proportion of studies using naturalistic and multiple methods increased from 13 percent to 44 percent by the late 1970s. These same trends can be observed in the research literature in general.

In many respects, the field was poised for the push into attempting analyses for more complex developmental patterns. Many realized that changes in the direction of multicausal models and research designs were necessary. However, it took the challenge of providing an adequate account of development in African-American communities, together with foundation and federal resources, to launch developmental psychology into a new era of research on social influences in development and ecological conceptualizations of the environment.

Conclusion and Implications

It is extremely difficult to establish causal determinants for such social historical events because factors that lead to paradigm shifts are complex and interactive (see Kuhn, 1970; Lakatos, 1970). Nevertheless, it is important to attempt to build a case with whatever evidence is available because failing to do so would, once again, relegate African-American participation in the events that shaped the nature of developmental inquiry to inconsequential roles and amount to a "whitewashing" of these significant historical events.

How are we to characterize the present state of developmental psychology? Several significant developmentalists view the field as highly fragmented and in a state of disarray (Bronfenbrenner, Kessel, Kessen, and White, 1986). Such portrayals, however, ignore significant changes in the constructs and research models that characterize the developmental enterprise over the period from the 1950s through the 1970s. In general terms, children are no longer viewed as the passive recipients of environmental forces that irrevocably shape the course of development but as active coparticipants in their own development. There is a general acceptance that in human development there are propensities for getting organized and finding order, which function adaptively across wide ranges of environmental variations. Moreover, there is a recognition that the child is open to learning, to constructing understandings and getting the meaning from social interpersonal systems as well as physical informational systems, at a much younger age than was ever before suspected.

The attention to the importance of context, of naturalistic observation; the use of more complex interactional research designs; and the concepts that have currency today have all received material and intellectual support from the revisions made to adequately apprehend and describe psychological development in African-American communities. Directly and indirectly, the study of African-American children has produced major changes in the methods and constructs of developmental psychology. Issues that were initally a peripheral concern for psychology, involving a marginal population and requiring only minor adjustments to procedures, have been incorporated into the conceptual mainstream of developmental psychology. A debt of recognition is owed to African-American children, in particular, and to those researchers who refused to quit, who resisted easy but inadequate formulations and had the intellectual integrity to persevere and modify their notions of development. Developmental psychology may seem to be adrift, attempting the complex task of synthesizing what has been learned from structural, functional, or contextual and neonativist accounts of development. However, Bronfenbrenner (see Bronfenbrenner, Kessel, Kessen, and White, 1986), sees a bright future emerging from the inclusion of more complex processes and ecological factors in development: "the beginning of a reintegration of what our field is about. . . . We are beginning to see complementarities between the affective, intellectual, and social aspects of developmental process" (p. 1224). If he is right, then we do indeed owe a significant debt to the study of African-American children, their families, and their communities.

References

Baratz, J. C. "Teaching Reading in an Urban Negro School System." In J. C. Baratz and R. W. Shuy (eds.), *Teaching Black Children to Read.* Washington, D.C.: Center for Applied Linguistics, 1969.

Bereiter, C., and Engelmann, S. *Teaching Disadvantaged Children in the Preschool.* Englewood Cliffs, N.J.: Prentice-Hall, 1966.

Berlin, B., Breedlove, D. E., and Raven, R. H. *Principles of Tzelthal Plant Classification: An Introduction to the Botanical Ethnography of a Mayan Speaking People of Highland Chipas.* San Diego: Academic Press, 1974.

Boyce, C. M. "Black Proficiency in Abstract Reasoning: A Test of Jensen's Two-Level Theory." Doctoral dissertation, Cornell University, 1983.

Bronfenbrenner, U., Kessel, F., Kessen, W., and White, S. "Toward a Critical Social History of Developmental Psychology: A Propaedeutic Discussion." *American Psychologist,* 1986, *41* (11), 1218-1230.

Bruner, J., Goodnow, J. J., and Austin, G. A. *A Study of Thinking.* New York: Wiley, 1956.

Carey, S. *Conceptual Change in Childhood.* Cambridge, Mass.: M.I.T. Press, 1985.

Case, R. *Intellectual Development: Birth to Adulthood.* San Diego: Academic Press, 1985.

Chomsky, N. *Syntactic Structures.* The Hague, Netherlands: Mouton, 1957.

Clark, K. B. "Effect of Prejudice and Discrimination on Personality Development." Paper presented at Midcentury White House Conference on Children and Youth, Washington, D.C., 1950.

Clark, K. *Prejudice and Your Child.* (2nd ed.) Boston, Mass.: Beacon Press, 1963.

Cole, M., and Bruner, J. "Cultural Differences and Inferences About Psychological Processes." *American Psychologist,* 1971, *26,* 867-876.

Gardner, H. *Frames of Mind: The Theory of Multiple Intelligences.* New York: Basic Books, 1983.

Gelman, R., and Baillargeon, R. "A Review of Some Piagetian Concepts." In J. H. Flavell and E. Markman (eds.), *Handbook of Child Psychology.* Vol. 3. New York: Wiley, 1983.

Ginsburg, H. *The Myth of the Deprived Child.* Englewood Cliffs, N.J.: Prentice-Hall, 1972.

Gladwin, T. *East Is a Big Bird.* Cambridge, Mass.: Harvard University Press, 1970.

Golden, M., and Birns, B. "Social Class and Cognitive Development in Infancy." *Merrill-Palmer Quarterly,* 1968, *14,* 139-149.

Gould, S. J. *The Panda's Thumb.* New York: Norton, 1980.

Gould, S. J. *The Mismeasure of Man.* New York: Norton, 1981.

Hess, R. D., and Shipman, V. "Early Experience and the Socialization of Cognitive Modes in Children." *Child Development,* 1965, *36,* 869-886.

Jensen, A. R. "How Much Can We Boost IQ and Scholastic Achievement." *Harvard Educational Review,* 1969, *39* (1), 1-123.

Keil, F. C. "Constraints on Knowledge and Cognitive Development." *Psychological Review*, 1981, *88* (3), 197-227.
Keil, F. C. "On the Structure-Dependent Nature of Stages of Cognitive Development." In I. Levin (ed.), *Stage and Structure*. Norwood, N.J.: Ablex, 1986.
Kuhn, D. "On the Dual Executive and Its Significance in the Development of Developmental Psychology." In D. Kuhn and J. Meacham (eds.), *On the Development of Developmental Psychology. VIII: Contributions to Human Development*. New York: Karger, 1983.
Kuhn, T. *The Structure of Scientific Revolutions*. (2nd ed.) Chicago: University of Chicago Press, 1970.
Laboratory of Comparative Human Cognition. "Culture and Intelligence." In R. J. Sternberg (ed.), *Handbook of Human Intelligence*. New York: Cambridge University Press, 1982.
Laboratory of Comparative Human Cognition. "Culture and Cognitive Development." In W. Kessen (ed.), *Mussen's Handbook of Child Psychology*, Vol. 1. New York: Wiley, 1983.
Labov, W. "The Logic of Nonstandard English." In *Georgetown Round Table on Language and Linguistics*. Washington, D.C.: Georgetown University Press, 1969.
Labov, W. *Language in the Inner City*. Philadelphia: University of Pennsylvania Press, 1972.
Lakatos, I. "Falsification and the Methodology of Scientific Research Programmes." In I. Lakatos and A. Musgrace (eds.), *Criticism and the Growth of Knowledge*. New York: Cambridge University Press, 1970.
Lakoff, G. *Women, Fire, and Dangerous Things: What Categories Reveal About the Mind*. Chicago: University of Chicago Press, 1987.
Lesser, G. S., Fifer, G., and Clark, D. H. "Mental Abilities of Children from Different Social-Class and Cultural Groups." *Monographs of the Society for Research in Child Development*, 1965, *30* (102), entire issue.
McCarthy, D. "Language Development in Children." In L. Carmichael, *Manual of Child Psychology*. (2nd ed.) New York: Wiley, 1954.
McLoyd, V. C., and Randolph, S. M. "Secular Trends in the Study of Afro-American Children: A Review of Child Development, 1936-1980." *Monographs of the Society for Research in Child Development*, 1985, *50* (4-5), 78-92.
Meacham, J. A. "Wisdom and the Context of Knowledge: Knowing That One Doesn't Know." In D. Kuhn and J. A. Meacham (eds.), *On the Development of Developmental Psychology. VIII: Contributions to Human Development*. New York: Karger, 1983.
Miller, G. A. "The Magic Number Seven, Plus or Minus Two: Some Limits on Our Capacity for Processing Information." *Psychological Review*, 1956, *63*, 81-97.
Miller-Jones, D. "Culture and Testing." *American Psychologist*, in press.
Neisser, U. "Toward an Ecologically Oriented Cognitive Science." In T. M. Schlechter and M. P. Toglia (eds.), *New Directions in Cognitive Science*. Norwood, N.J.: Ablex, 1985.
Neisser, U. (ed.). *The School Achievement of Minority Children: New Perspectives*. Hillsdale, N.J.: Erlbaum, 1986.
Newell, A., Shaw, J. C., and Simon, H. A. "Elements of a Theory of Human Problem Solving." *Psychological Review*, 1958, *65*, 151-166.
Piaget, J. *The Origins of Intelligence in Children*. New York: International Universities Press, 1952.
Piaget, J. "Piaget's Theory." In P. H. Mussen (ed.), *Carmichael's Manual of Child*

Psychology. Vol. 1. New York: Wiley, 1970.
Riegel, K. F. "An Epitaph for Paradigm." *Human Development*, 1973, *16* (1), 1-7.
Rosch, E. "Cognitive Representations of Semantic Categories." *Journal of Experimental Psychology General*, 1975, *104*, 192-233.
Samelson, F. "On the Science and Politics of IQ." *Social Research*, 1975, *42*, 467-488.
Scribner, S. and Cole, M. *The Psychology of Literacy*. Cambridge, Mass.: Harvard University Press, 1981.
Shweder, R. A., and LeVine, R. A. *Culture Theory: Essays on Mind, Self, and Emotion*. New York: Cambridge University Press, 1984.
Sternberg, R. J. *Human Abilities: An Information-Processing Approach*. New York: W. H. Freeman, 1985.
Stodolsky, S. S., and Lesser, G. "Learning Patterns in the Disadvantaged." *Harvard Educational Review*, 1967, *37*, 546-593.
Tulkin, S. R. "An Analysis of the Concept of Cultural Deprivation." *Developmental Psychology*, 1972, 6 (2), 326-339.
U.S. Department of Health, Education, and Welfare, National Institute of Child Health and Human Development. *Perspectives on Human Deprivation: Biological, Psychological, and Sociological*. Washington, D.C.: U.S. Department of Health, Education, and Welfare, 1968.
Wachs, T. D., Uzgiris, I. C., and Hunt, J.M.V. "Cognitive Development in Infants of Different Age Levels and from Different Environmental Backgrounds: An Explanatory Investigation." *Merrill-Palmer Quarterly*, 1971, *17*, 283-317.
Wertsch, J. V., and Youniss, J. "Contextualizing the Investigation: The Case of Developmental Psychology." *Human Development*, 1987, *30*, 18-31.
Whorf, B. L. *Language, Thought, and Reality*. Cambridge, Mass.: M.I.T. Press, 1956.

Dalton Miller-Jones is associate professor of developmental psychology at the City University of New York Graduate School and University Center.

Concern for the welfare of Blacks played a major role in strengthening ties between the fields of child development and social policy over the past twenty-five years since the Moynihan report. However, the interests of Black children are often obscured by the emphasis on economic deprivation instead of on race and racism in the formulation of social policy and by implementation of policy in ways that undermine the survival strategies of poor Black families.

Historical and Contemporary Linkages Between Black Child Development and Social Policy

Valora Washington

From conception to adolescence, Black children face harsh challenges to their growth and survival because of race and regardless of social class (McAdoo and McAdoo, 1985; Children's Defense Fund, 1985). Chief among the problems is persistent poverty. Almost half of Black children are poor, and about 90 percent of persistently poor children are Black. Compared with White children, Black children are two and one-half times more likely to live in substandard housing and five times more likely to be dependent on welfare (Children's Defense Fund, 1985). Consequently, Black children, more than any other group, are particularly affected by social policy.

Yet, despite the voluminous body of literature about Black children and the urgent need to assist them, few scholars have addressed specifically the links between the status of Black children, research, and social policy. In this chapter, I examine some of the historical and contemporary linkages between Black children and social policy. I argue that, despite the prevalent presentation of statistics about Black children in

D. T. Slaughter (ed.). *Black Children and Poverty: A Developmental Perspective.*
New Directions for Child Development, no. 42. San Francisco: Jossey-Bass, Winter 1988.

policy contexts, the real needs and interests of these children are often obscured. Furthermore, I argue that, in critical ways, the advent of the subdiscipline of child development and social policy itself can be traced to early efforts to link basic child development research and the experiences of poor Black children. Given the paradox of the obscurity of Black children in social policy and the focus on Black and minority children in the scholarly arena dealing with social policy, I speculate on future ties between child development and social policy as these ties address Black children in poverty.

Contributions of Black Children

The history of Black child development research, particularly as it relates to public policy, has received little attention. Some authors have asserted that the advent of the Office of Economic Opportunity and Project Head Start in 1965 represents the entry date of Blacks in the early childhood and child development fields. In 1975, Edwards stated that Blacks had only recently begun to conduct social science research and to be represented in the literature on early childhood. Yet, as Cunningham and Osborn (1979) have pointed out, there was a continued interest in child development among Blacks long before the Office of Economic Opportunity was established.

Too often, Black children and their families have been ignored in research. In a review of the contents of five sociology, five social work, and three Black journals from 1965 to 1968, Johnson (1981) found that empirical articles on Black families made up only 1 percent of all articles and only 3 percent of all empirical articles. Similarly, Super (1982) found that, except for a period during the 1960s when some studies included participants from diverse social, economic, and racial backgrounds, most research published in *Child Development* from 1930 to 1979 was on middle-class Whites.

According to Staples and Mirande (1980), the 1970s represented the most productive period of Black family research in history. More than fifty books and 500 articles about Black family life were published during the decade. This production represented a 500 percent increase over the amount of literature on the Black family published in all years before 1970.

Where it existed, research on Black children has typically advanced misconceptions and misinterpretations about them. Deficit interpretations of their language, behavior, and abilities evolved as a natural consequence of race-comparative studies. Studies that include only Blacks in the sample may also reflect a deficit orientation. McLoyd and Randolph (1984), in their content analysis of empirical studies on Black children in major journals from 1973 to 1975, found that studies comparing Black children with other groups were not more likely to expouse an explicit deficit model. The authors concluded that race-homogeneous studies may implicitly involve race comparisons and that race-comparative studies often appear to be atheoretical, reporting race differences of little informative value.

McLoyd and Randolph (1985) also examined the changing nature of studies published in *Child Development* between 1936 and 1980 in which Black children were compared with other groups or constituted the entire sample. Studies were grouped into four time periods: 1936-1965, 1966-1970, 1971-1975, and 1976-1980. McLoyd and Randolph found that the frequency of both types of studies peaked during 1971-1975, specifically in 1971. There was a steady decline across the four periods in the tendency of studies to have race or ethnicity mentioned in the abstract.

Although the relative number of studies mentioning Black children and families may be small, research on Black children seems to have had a disproportionate impact on the relationship between child development research and social policy in recent decades. Pizzo (1983) noted that federal policy between 1900-1929 concentrated on White children; Black families lived primarily in the rural Southeast and outside the typical sphere of the socially conscious policy shapers. In contrast, federal policy from 1960 to 1979 had strong racial overtones; debates about federal responsibility versus states' rights appeared to reflect sentiment that racial minorities had been conceded too much, as presumably illustrated by the growth of public assistance programs.

Three areas of research illustrate the importance of studies on Black children in shaping the advent of the subdiscipline of research and social policy: intelligence testing and assessment; preschool development and education, as illustrated by Project Head Start; and improvements in elementary and secondary education fostered by compensatory education programs.

Intelligence Testing and Assessment. Miller-Jones, in Chapter Five, has pointed out that early research in the 1960s suggested that Black children had intellectual "deficits" in the perceptual, cognitive, and linguistic areas. Laosa (1984) has asserted that the history of U.S. social policies toward children is closely intertwined with the history of intelligence testing. Arguments about "innate" racial differences were used to rationalize many policies, including the passage of racist immigration laws, school segregation, and ability grouping in educational institutions. Furthermore, allegations resulting from racial bias in intelligence tests have formed the bases of a series of policy actions by the judicial, legislative, and executive branches of government as well as by professional associations.

Preschool Development and Education. Extrapolating from environmentalist ideas about the role of experience in the development of intellect, psychologists began to link Black children's low scores on IQ and achievement tests to the lack of intellectual stimulation in the home. This may explain part of the increase in research on preschoolers published in *Child Development* between 1966 and 1975. Based partly on these ideas, federal policy in this period sought to alleviate the intellectual and social deficits of the poor through a variety of parent and child improvement programs, such as Head Start.

Project Head Start, *the* major federal child development program, is a comprehensive effort to provide health, educational, and social services to preschool children and their families. About 42 percent of Head Start children are Black, and about two-thirds of the children are members of ethnic minority groups.

Consequently, Head Start/preschool-intervention research and public policy have particularly strong relationships to Black children. Not surprisingly, issues of cultural diversity surfaced in the early days of Head Start and other intervention programs. For example, the desegregation requirements for Head Start grant eligibility provoked some initial resentment of Head Start programs in several southern states. Despite parental and community enthusiasm for the goals of Head Start, the program has been criticized for the ethnic composition of its staffing patterns, particularly in supervisory positions. It has also been charged that Head Start has promulgated a deficit view of Black children and their families and communities (see Washington and Oyemade, 1987). Furthermore, although the major studies and reports on the effectiveness of preschool intervention have extensively used Black children as subjects, these studies have considerably less representation and visibility of Black scholars (see Cole and Washington, 1986).

Compensatory Education. Preschool intervention programs like Head Start have enjoyed widespread popularity but have not achieved equal educational opportunity (Slaughter, 1982). By the mid 1970s, there was growing cynicism about the marriage of child development research and public policy: The school performance of Black children had not changed dramatically, critics were questioning programs conceived for minorities by the White majority, and theories of social inequality challenged the deficit assumptions of most social programs. Jensen (1969) concluded that the programs had failed because Blacks are not only culturally deprived but also genetically inferior.

Many academics disputed theories of genetic differences, but persistent poverty and racial disparities fueled the growing conviction that something even more basic than cultural deprivation was "wrong" with Black people: It was widely asserted that "compensatory education" was called for, that is, early intervention tailored to limited intellectual capacities and using the rote-learning strategies for which Blacks were said to be better suited. So, for different reasons, American academics and the federal government supported additional remedial programs designed to change the way Blacks learn and think (Mitchell, 1982).

The reassessment of research and social policy in the 1970s led to the passage of several compensatory education programs. The Elementary and Secondary School Act was passed, and Project Head Start was initiated, in 1965. The Coleman report (Coleman and others, 1966) appeared in 1966. "Sesame Street" began in 1969, and 1969 through 1970 marked the largest wave of court-ordered desegregation in the South.

For example, today, approximately 40 percent of the budget of the U.S. Department of Education is allocated to provide direct services for "disadvantaged" elementary and secondary school children (William T. Grant Foundation, 1987). The major programs are Project Follow-Through and Chapter 1 of the Education Consolidation and Improvement Act. About 29 percent of Chapter 1 students are Black, and 16 percent are Hispanic (Riddle, 1986). Data on improved reading and mathematics achievement of Blacks suggest that Chapter 1 is effective (see Jones, 1983; for a contrary view, see Jensen, 1985).

Yet compensatory education programs have been the object of much criticism and analysis. For example, in a poignant essay, Mitchell (1982) has described her experiences as a teacher in a compensatory preschool program and as a graduate student and researcher. She found the compensatory program to be "patronizing" and to have an "implicit denigration of the milieu of Black culture."

Furthermore, the assessment procedures used to determine a child's need for compensatory education often have been viewed as biased contributors to improper classification and labeling of Black children (Laosa, 1984). The consequence, according to some observers, is reflected in facts such as those indicating that a Black child is more than three times as likely to be classified as educable mentally retarded and twice as likely to be classified as trainable mentally retarded or seriously emotionally disturbed (Children's Defense Fund, 1985).

Bereiter (1985) observed that, for two decades, continual acrimony has characterized the debate about the explanations for educational disadvantage. He noted that much of the sensitivity on this topic results from the focus on students identified demographically, such as by race. Although "things are much calmer on the educational disadvantage front today" (Bereiter, 1985, p. 540), the issues are being avoided, not resolved.

The two primary retreats from the issues are the movement toward individual, rather than categorical, diagnosis and prescription and the movement toward nonspecific compensatory education based on empirical generalizations about what is required to improve instruction for historically low-achieving groups. In the former view, for example, the educationally disadvantaged are not defined conceptually but are simply those children who have traditionally been regarded as suitable candidates for compensatory education.

Obscurity of Black Children in Social Policy

Although Black child research has been a relatively small part of the field of child development, the most public and controversial issues in child development—intelligence testing, preschool programs, and compensatory education—have strong racial overtones. Consequently, media, scholarly, and legislative accounts on the status of children typically present a mass of race-comparative information that creates an initial impression that special attention is being given to Black or minority children. Yet the needs and interests of Black children are often obscured in two particularly important ways: by the emphasis on economic deprivation as opposed to race and racism in the formulation of social policy and by the implementation of social policy in ways that undermine the survival strategies of poor Black families.

Race and Social Policy. Social welfare policy has been based on the premise that, if poor people were provided with food, housing, and income, they would eventually become self-sufficient. However, in addition to economic deprivations, a substantial number of welfare recipients must confront racial discrimination. Social welfare policy has not circumvented this additional barrier to self-sufficiency. By focusing on economic deprivations only, social policy fails to (1) consider the historical salience of race with regard to social class, (2) respond to the demographic characteristics of the recipients of public assistance, (3) balance competing interests that impinge on Black child and family issues, (4) acknowledge and eliminate the racism inherent in the distinction between the "deserving" and "undeserving" poor, and (5) consider the interests and needs of Black children in the implementation of policy.

Race and Social Class. Both child development research and policy have promulgated a poverty-centered approach as it relates to Black children. This is illustrated by the fact that the number of articles in *Child Development* on Black children from low-income backgrounds increased from 1936–1965 to 1966–1975 and that this focus remained stable and high during the subsequent periods (McLoyd and Randolph, 1985).

A poverty-centered approach to development and analysis of public policy fails to consider that African-Americans have a peculiar history in the United States that may provide insight into the causes, consequences, and cures of their impoverishment. This ahistorical perspective glosses over the fact that attention to race has been normative in American life. A major assumption of this "color-blind" approach is that the problems of Black people can be solved in the same way as the problems of impoverished Whites. This ahistorical perspective can lead to social policy solutions that are indifferent to the fact that the poverty of Blacks often results from political and economic systems that condone and foster institutional racism.

Demographic Characteristics of Public Assistance Recipients. The continuing importance of race is graphically illustrated in a review of the demographic characteristics of public assistance recipients. Black children are more than three times more likely than White children to be poor, 42 percent versus 13.4 percent, respectively. For example, in 1969, 19.1 percent of Blacks and 3.6 percent of Whites were on welfare. By 1979, the proportions of Blacks and Whites on welfare had risen to 28.1 percent and 5.3 percent, respectively. Today, Black children are five times as likely to be dependent on welfare; about two of every five Black children are on Aid to Families with Dependent Children (AFDC) (Children's Defense Fund, 1985). Consequently Black children and families have long been disproportionately represented in federally sponsored income assistance programs (Washington, 1985).

In fact, negative public opinion may partly result from rapid growth of welfare assistance and the unanticipated "profile" of welfare recipients (Steiner, 1976). The AFDC program was established to benefit widows with children or the wives and children of disabled fathers. This was, in fact, the case until the 1950s. By 1980, only about 4 percent of the fathers of AFDC recipients were deceased or disabled. Now the enormous growth in welfare caseloads stems from female-headed households that exist as a result of divorce or the nonformation of families, a phenomenon particularly marked in the Black community (Washington, 1984).

However, all of the stigma associated with welfare programs cannot be wholly due to these trends in the demographic characteristics of welfare recipients. As will be shown later, racism was prevalent even as these programs were on the drawing board.

Therefore, a proper analysis of America's poor people and any restructuring of federal programs related to the poor should respond to these demographic trends. These trends underscore the importance of specifically considering the application of federal programs to the needs of Black children.

Balancing Competing Interests. The clash of competing interests in policy arenas during discussion of welfare policies has not been productive for Black children. Relating government action to family stability has never been fashionable in America (Steiner, 1981). Nevertheless, various policy initiatives have been proposed, as illustrated by the controversial Moynihan report (1965) and the Family Assistance Plan (FAP) (see Washington, 1985).

The Moynihan report concluded that the Black family was at the heart of the deterioration of African-American society. Further labeling the Black family as a tangle of pathology, Moynihan called for federal intervention in Black family life. Blacks and Whites angrily charged Moynihan with blaming the victims for the poverty and racism they suffer. Steiner (1981) observed that, within the context of a civil rights initiative, Moynihan's suggestions for strengthening the family imputed a collective abnormality to some Black activists and intellectuals.

Nixon's Family Assistance Plan was a guaranteed income concept that was expected to simplify the welfare system and expand public assistance to many people who were ineligible under the AFDC program (singles, childless couples, and married couples without children). Yet, in 1968, the guaranteed income idea was overwhelmingly opposed by Whites and favored by Blacks.

Many supporters of the plan felt that FAP would fuel political and economic independence for Black southern workers who had to settle for low-paying and irregular part-time jobs. Yet most Black members of Congress, the welfare-rights community, and other liberals objected to FAP on the basis that it (1) might force poor homemakers into the underpaid workforce, (2) did not provide an income equal to the income at the poverty line, (3) would change the demographic character of public assistance recipients from 81 percent female-headed families and 50 percent Black to 61 percent White and half male, (4) provided the same income to a family of four that a needy elderly couple would receive from old-age benefits, and (5) would not increase benefits to urban northerners.

In the process of FAP's defeat, none of the several alternatives to FAP, including one led by Black members of Congress, were formally considered (Bowler, 1974). Clearly, effective formulation of social welfare policy requires that competing regional and racial interests receive careful consideration.

The Deserving and Undeserving Poor. Part of the difficulty in balancing competing interests lies in the notion that relief should not be made available to all poor people; rather, aid should be provided only to selected categories of those deserving poor who are poor through no fault of their own. This view partly reflects the Victorian attitude that poverty is the result of individual handicaps and deficiencies. Victorian philanthropists believed that unrestricted and unregulated charity caused poverty and weakened the moral fiber of poor people (see Washington, 1985).

Current welfare rhetoric continues to have a basis in the distinction between the deserving and undeserving poor. Thus, rehabilitation and opportunities programs and welfare reform typically focus on changing individuals.

Cultural Diversity and Policy Implementation

In addition to its failure to address race and racism, social policy obscures the interests and needs of Black children in the implementation of policy. The expressed goal of social welfare policy—to promote healthy and stable family life—can be undermined by legislators seeking to deny benefits to certain groups, by state or federal eligibility criteria, or by operational definitions of the family. Furthermore, because of the diversity of families, social policies affect different families in different ways.

In AFDC, the needs and interest of Black children are further obscured by policies that fail to consider diverse perspectives on family structure and functioning, perspectives revealed in contemporary child development and family research (see Washington and LaPoint, in press). Consequently, social policy has not always adapted to the survival needs of Black children.

Policies that imply a nuclear-family structure would affect Black and White families differently simply because more Black families represent the extended-family form (Hill, 1972). Both poor and middle-class Black children are more likely than White children to live in multigenerational households. The extended family is essential, in part, to compensate for the impact of social policy failures on the Black community, specifically low AFDC payments and high unemployment (see Washington and LaPoint, in press).

Furthermore, housing policies and sizes, for example, make it difficult for three-generation families to live together (Moroney, 1977). One Black grandmother who absorbed two families into her household as a way of adapting to the death of her two sons was arrested and fined for violating a city housing ordinance in Cleveland, Ohio. The case was not resolved until it reached the U.S. Supreme Court, where it was argued persuasively that constitutional protection of the family extends beyond the arbitrary boundaries of the nuclear family.

Another area of cultural difference involves child custody. Informal adoptions of young relatives occur in about 13 percent of Black families, compared with 3 percent of White families (Hill, 1972). Most of these Black children are absorbed into their grandmothers' families; Black elderly women have the highest rate of absorption of all other groups, regardless of race or sex. Yet community practices concerning the transfer of children have often conflicted with state laws.

Prospects for the Future

Both scholarly and policy interests in ethnic differences have long and peculiar histories. The objectivity of science has been unquestionably influenced by the changing political and economic climate of the nation. In its heyday, research on the development of Black children effectively challenged barriers to social and educational equality, as in the 1954 *Brown* v. *Board of Education* decision and the evolution of Project Head Start.

Yet much of the research on Black children's development, with its orientation toward poverty and social problems, lacks clarity, specificity, and relevance to formulation of policy and delivery of service. The sheer volume of the literature and the narrow focus of much of it leave many potential users confused or immobilized. The implications for parents, teachers, service providers, or policymakers are often shrouded with inconclusiveness, rhetoric, and contradictions.

Nevertheless, this chapter shows that the study of Black children has been a significant force in efforts to link child development research and public policy. Although Black children constitute perhaps the largest group of minors affected by public policy, their specific needs and interests are often obscured.

I think that the relative absence of Blacks as child development researchers and as policymakers is directly related to this state of affairs. Legislators and scholars who have neither experienced nor, in some cases, exposed themselves to cultural diversity are ill-prepared to weigh ethnicity as one evaluative criterion important to their work. Thus, productive efforts to establish liaisons between research and public policy must include active participation by social scientists and legislators from Black and other ethnic groups.

Mitchell (1982) has noted that social scientists are often uncertain of the influence they wield and even uncomfortable when research provides the justification for a great many of the social policies enacted in this country. This is particularly true for Black researchers who, because of their status, may be haunted by particular questions and contradictions. For example, Black researchers are expected to be objective social scientists, yet have a Black perspective. They may interact more with the White power structure and less with their ethnic communities; the result is a state of "double marginality." They chose careers in research as a vehicle for effecting social change, but must be careful that their work and ethnicity are not exploited. Finally, they must consider the consequences of making public "shared secrets."

Yet social scientists have the potential to contribute a great deal to the discussion of persistent poverty among Black children. The generation of knowledge about this population can effectively dispel myths, promote understanding, indicate policy alternatives, and stimulate advances to the general public welfare, provided deficit-oriented research paradigms are abandoned (Washington, 1984).

Although developmental studies now give more emphasis to the cultural, ecological, social, and interdisciplinary contexts of human development, applications of this knowledge to the general social welfare do not necessarily reflect these recent trends. Consequently, deficit views of poor families and children have historically played an influential role in the interpretation of their behavior and development.

In the future, addressing the issues of poverty among Black children will continue to be an essential task of our time—a task that is imperative for all Americans, not just Black parents or Black scholars. In the next decade, there will be a dramatic increase in the number of children in the United States, a larger proportion of whom will be Blacks, or members of other ethnic minorities, and poor. For example, the Census Bureau's 12 percent growth projection for 1985 to 2000 includes increases of 23 percent among Blacks and 9 percent for Whites (see Washington and LaPoint, in press).

Clearly America is becoming more diverse, not more homogeneous. Consequently, Black children represent an underdeveloped resource that will become increasingly important to the nation's economic, military, and political strength (see Washington and LaPoint, in press).

Black children and youth are an equally important barometer of the status of the Black population. Indeed, almost one-third of Black people are less than sixteen years old. In addition, the number of Blacks eighteen to twenty-four years old has increased at almost twice the rate of Whites in that age group. Consequently, the overall well-being of Black children is vital to the health and future of the Black community.

Future ties between Black child development research and social policy may be enhanced by several factors. First, research that neither denigrates Black children as a result of their status in American society nor idealizes them in the process of maintaining myths about Black family life and survival is needed. Second, both research and policy would benefit from efforts to delineate and emphasize the traditional values that have been found to foster achievement (that is, work, ethnic pride, discipline, persistence, religion, caring, faith, self-confidence, and independence). Government can support Blacks' reemphasis of their traditional values in several ways. Full, nondiscriminatory employment of Black parents at decent wage levels would do much to support this goal.

Third, we must recognize that the opportunities for Black children will become more widely divergent. Those children in families who are highly skilled or well educated may see an unlimited future and prosperity. On the other hand, children of the poor or of single or adolescent parents are likely to become increasingly alienated and distant from mainstream American life. Research and policy should investigate the possibilities suggested by these differences.

Fourth, although Black families and Black communities can do and are doing a great deal to extend the opportunities for Black children, comprehensive public action that uses research resources is necessary to address persistent poverty. Yet, despite strong political rhetoric about the value of children and families, there is little in American social policy, aside from the public schools, that gives national priority to allocating the resources of the United States to fulfill these lofty promises for children and families. The contrast between political and academic rhetoric poses an American dilemma that surrounds public policy toward children.

References

Bereiter, C. "The Changing Face of Educational Disadvantagement." *Phi Delta Kappan*, 1985, *66*, 538-541.

Bowler, M. K. *The Nixon Guaranteed Income Proposal.* Cambridge, Mass.: Ballinger, 1974.
Brown v. Board of Education, Topeka, Kansas. 347 U.S. 483 (1954).
Children's Defense Fund. *Black and White Children in America: Key Facts.* Washington, D.C.: Children's Defense Fund, 1985.
Cole, O. J., and Washington, V. "A Critical Analysis of the Effects of Head Start on Minority Children." *Journal of Negro Education,* 1986, *55,* 91-106.
Coleman, J. S., Campbell, E. Q., Hobson, C. J., McPartland, J., Mood, A. M., Weinfeld, F. D., and York, R. L. *Equality of Educational Opportunity.* Washington, D.C.: U.S. Government Printing Office, 1966.
Cunningham, C. E., and Osborn, D. K. "A Historical Examination of Blacks in Early Childhood Education." *Young Children,* Mar. 1979, pp. 20-29.
Edwards, R. M. "Race and Class in Early Childhood Education." *Young Children,* Sept. 1975, pp. 401-411.
Hill, R. *The Strengths of Black Families.* New York: Emerson-Hall, 1972.
Jensen, A. R. "How Much Can We Boost IQ and Scholastic Achievement?" *Harvard Educational Review,* 1969, *39* (1), 1-123.
Jensen, A. R. "Compensatory Education and the Theory of Intelligence." *Phi Delta Kappan,* 1985, *66,* 554-558.
Johnson, L. B. "Perspectives on Black Family Empirical Research: 1965-1978." In H. P. McAdoo (ed.), *Black Families.* Newbury Park, Calif.: Sage, 1981.
Jones, L. V. *White-Black Achievement Differences: The Narrowing Gap.* Washington, D.C.: Science and Public Policy Seminars of the Federation of Behavioral, Psychological, and Cognitive Sciences, 1983.
Laosa, L. M. "Social Policies Toward Children of Diverse Ethnic, Racial, and Language Groups in the United States." In H. W. Stevenson and A. E. Siegel (eds.), *Child Development Research and Social Policy.* Chicago: University of Chicago Press, 1984.
McAdoo, H. P., and McAdoo, J. L. (eds.). *Black Children: Social, Educational, and Parental Environments.* Newbury Park, Calif.: Sage, 1985.
McLoyd, V. C., and Randolph, S. M. "The Conduct and Publication of Research on Afro-American Children: A Content Analysis." *Human Development,* 1984, *27,* 65-75.
McLoyd, V. C., and Randolph, S. M. "Secular Trends in the Study of Afro-American Children: A Review of Child Development 1936-1980." *Monographs of the Society for Research in Child Development,* 1985, *50,* (4-5), 78-92.
Mitchell, J. "Reflections of a Black Social Scientist: Some Struggles, Some Doubts, Some Hopes." *Harvard Educational Review,* 1982, *52,* 27-44.
Moroney, R. M. "The Need for a National Family Policy." *Urban and Social Change,* 1977, *10,* 10-14.
Moynihan, D. P. *The Negro Family: The Case for National Action.* Washington, D.C.: Office of Policy Planning and Research, U.S. Department of Labor, 1965.
Pizzo, P. "Slouching Toward Bethlehem: American Federal Policy Perspectives on Children and Their Families." In E. F. Zigler, S. L. Kagan, and E. Klugman (eds.), *Children, Families, and Government Perspectives on American Social Policy.* New York: Cambridge University Press, 1983.
Riddle, W. C. *Education for Disadvantaged Children: Federal Aid. Updated 03/26/86.* Washington, D.C.: Congressional Research Service, 1986.
Slaughter, D. T. "What Is the Future of Head Start?" *Young Children,* March 1982, pp. 3-9.
Staples, R., and Mirande, A. "Racial and Cultural Variations Among American Families: A Decennial Review." *Journal of Marriage and the Family.* 1980, *42,*

157-173.
Steiner, G. Y. *The Children's Cause.* Washington, D.C.: The Brookings Institution, 1976.
Steiner, G. Y. *The Futility of Family Policy.* Washington, D.C.: The Brookings Institution, 1981.
Super, C. M. "Secular Trends in Child Development and the Institutionalization of Professional Disciplines." *Newsletter of the Society for Research in Child Development,* Spring 1982, pp. 10–11.
Washington, V. "Continuity of Care in American Support for Dependent Children: The AFDC Example." *International Journal of Mental Health,* 1984, *12,* 59–77.
Washington, V. "Social Policy, Cultural Diversity, and the Obscurity of Black Children." *Journal of Educational Equity and Leadership,* 1985, *5,* 320–335.
Washington, V., and LaPoint, V. *Black Children and American Institutions: An Ecological Review and Resource Guide.* New York: Garland, in press.
Washington, V., and Oyemade, U. J. *Project Head Start: Past, Present, and Future Trends in the Context of Family Needs.* New York: Garland, 1987.
William T. Grant Foundation, Commission on Work, Family, and Citizenship. *Current Federal Policies and Programs for Youth.* New York: William T. Grant Foundation, 1987.

Valora Washington is professor and vice-president/dean of faculty at Antioch College, Yellow Springs, Ohio. She is a member of the Social Policy Committee of the Society for Research in Child Development.

Part 3.

Epilogue

Implications of focusing on adaptive coping for schooling and related educational interventions with impoverished Black children are discussed.

Black Children, Schooling, and Educational Interventions

Diana T. Slaughter

The late Allison Davis was a social anthropologist who applied his scholarly training and knowledge to the field of education and child development. When he wrote and published *Children of Bondage* (Davis and Dollard, [1948] 1964) and *Social-Class Influences upon Learning* (Davis, 1948) in the 1940s, he stressed that the social classes were cultures that, through the resultant community-familial interactive processes, had independent lives of their own, lives that would be perpetuated across time through intergenerational transmission (socialization) within families. One of the architects of the theoretical underpinnings of the War on Poverty, Davis persistently underestimated the adaptive, positive coping capacities of the lower classes. Furthermore, he, like many others of his time, was convinced by his own research findings that race, by comparison with social class, was a minimally influential factor in human psychological development (Slaughter and McWorter, 1985).

On balance today, it seems that there are strengths and weaknesses associated with the cultures of all social-class groupings and that race and racism are important moderating variables in theory and research in human development, but it is not always obvious how they will affect behavior. For example, cultural attitudes toward race, and racism, may condition attitudes toward utilization of schooling as a vehicle of upward mobility (see Chapter One in this volume), but evaluative judgments about race are not predictive of self-esteem (see Chapter Four). In the areas of language and speech, not race but the cultures conditioning race influence behavior and development (see Chapters Two, Three, and Five). On other occasions, the dismissal of race and racism would result in our ignoring the disproportionate impact of economic conditions on Black children (see the Editor's Notes) and, therefore, limited tailoring of possible policy-oriented solutions to the needs and interests of Black children and their families (see Chapter Six). What roles do psychologists concerned with individual education and development have in helping to redefine or identify the effective environments of Black children?

Developmental Psychology and the Public Interest

Since the late sixties, there has been an active debate within the American Psychological Association as to psychologists' roles in public policy. The focus of that debate has primarily been on how psychological research findings can contribute positively not just to advancement of knowledge but also to the general human welfare (for example, Ramey, 1974; Reppucci and Kirk, 1984). Roles for psychologists in the public arena have been described. These include expert witness, translator and consultant, administrator, activist-collaborator, social engineer, and, of course, most typically, researcher or policy evaluator.

In the role of researcher or policy evaluator, the psychologist may help to destroy stereotypes and myths about policies, programs, and/or populations. Studies of American minority-group children and families, particularly Black American children and families, have frequently dispelled myths about these populations. Many believe that study findings also compel reassessment of existing developmental research paradigms, as earlier findings seemed to highlight only deficits, deviance, and pathological problems within Black communities.

According to McLoyd and Randolph (1984), in recent years developmental studies in psychology that used race-comparative research designs were no more likely to signal deficit-oriented paradigms than were studies that used race-homogeneous or race-heterogeneous designs. However, given the history of how the study of Black children and families initially arose, this finding is not surprising. Slaughter and McWorter (1985) have argued that Blacks began to be studied in the mid to late thirties not in an effort to further characterize the nature of human development and behavior but as part of a desire to assimilate these new urban migrants into mainstream American society. At that time, consideration of the general welfare of Blacks did not include consideration of any cultural context that the larger American society would be obligated to respect.

Research in developmental psychology had to change in several significant respects for the strengths of the population to be revealed. First, as Reppucci (1985) has suggested, it had to become less person centered and thereby give more emphasis to the cultural-ecological, as well as social, contexts in which individual development occurs. Second, it had to assume an interdisciplinary perspective, including not only key concepts from the other social science disciplines, such as sociology, anthropology, and history, but also biomedical and humanistic perspectives. Third, it had to emphasize research designs and data gathering strategies that are more naturalistic and field centered, as well as qualitative, in contrast to more traditional laboratory or experimental, quantitatively oriented researches. Most importantly, it had to select research questions, theoretical perspectives, and problems of interest to the population being studied. Therefore, the studies are more likely to have an applied focus. In fact, assuming that the ultimate goal of such psychological studies is to improve the lives of children, the distinction between basic and applied research is not perceived to be especially useful.

I also believe that in the future the nature of cross-cultural psychological research will be affected significantly by these trends. As behavioral scientists, rather than simply using such field studies as laboratories to validate or test the universality of theories or propositions about American children and families (see Wagner, 1986), we will also stress similarities and differences in the experiences of children and families in racial and ethnic minorities worldwide.

This volume originated from a symposium that I was invited to convene and chair on the contributions of research on minority children to the field of child development. I decided to focus on obtaining critical summaries of issues and findings in particular areas—those in which deficit-oriented paradigms had played, and some would say continue to play, a particularly influential role in the interpretation of Black behavior and development. In recent years, we have witnessed a revival of deficit-oriented paradigms, originally begun around the time of the Moynihan (1965) report, within the traditional social sciences, including psychology, sociology, and anthropology. Even face-to-face contact with respondents appears not to attenuate the possibility of overemphasis on their weaknesses, as contrasted with their strengths. This occurs, in part, because use of a particular research strategy or technique does not of itself guarantee that the data obtained will be interpreted so as not to completely blame the victim (Ryan, 1971), err by absolving the victim of all responsibility for improving conditions, or undermine the potency of previously identified strengths of the victims by stressing only how these strengths are used in truly deviant or pathological situations.

In sharp contrast, writing to Division 37 of the American Psychological Association, Bronfenbrenner (1986) has recently presented an excellent analysis of children in poverty in the 1980s, an analysis that offers the possibility for adaptive, positive coping, even given considerable environmental stress, for Black children and their families. Bronfenbrenner reported that between 1962 to 1969 impoverished Black children, during a period of relative national economic prosperity, were significantly more likely than impoverished White children to leave poverty, particularly Black children from two-parent families. However, over a longer time span, 1959 to 1984, children, particularly children less than six years old and especially Black children, have replaced older adults in being disproportionately at risk of poverty. Arguing that poverty is not a Black or a White problem, but an American problem requiring national solutions, Bronfenbrenner (1986, p. 2) stated: "Today, parents of 13.4 million children under 18 have to make do with an income that averages $4000 below the poverty line. And although the poverty rate is much higher for black families than for white, the overwhelming majority of poor children in our nation are white, in a ratio of almost 2 to 1 (8.5 vs 4.4 million). Clearly this is not a black problem, nor a white problem. It is an American problem, and requires an American solution." Similar analyses have been made by Pearce and McAdoo (1981), Edelman (1987), Moynihan (1986), and Duncan (personal communication, April 29, 1988).

According to Bronfenbrenner, research indicates that apart from economic conditions, other factors can affect how environments affect psychological functioning, including human growth and development. Major changes in family ecology, as well as persistently negative or positive social ecologies, can profoundly affect human development (Elder, 1974; Elder, Van Nguyen, and Caspi, 1985). Furthermore, as Bronfenbrenner noted, the impact of such environmental stresses will vary, depending on the psychological characteristics of the persons and groups affected and whether the changes permit minimum-level adaptations within family relations. Additionally, I believe that whenever a human group endures persistent economic and social deprivations, the long-term physical and psychological survival of its members is contingent on that group's ability to generate and sustain regulatory sociocultural values and norms that are transmitted from generation to generation and are aimed at positive, adaptive coping. These crucial assumptions undergird the arguments of all contributors to this volume.

Educational Intervention and Schooling

In America, familial changes have been dramatic in the past twenty years. Apart from those changes in families that seem to affect the entire population (for example, increases in divorce rates, single-parent families, and numbers of working women with young children) many have particularly affected Black families. For Blacks, for example, the prevalence of single-parent households increased from 21 percent to 44 percent between 1960 and 1980. As these households are disproportionately at risk for poverty (Pearce and McAdoo, 1981), it is likely that significantly more Blacks than Whites experience enduring poverty across generations. Corcoran, Duncan, Gurin, and Gurin (1985) have demonstrated that the majority of the American population is unlikely to ever remain in poverty beyond three to five years. However, according to Swinton (1988, p. 136), Census Bureau statistics indicate that "the national poverty rate for Black persons in 1986 was 31.1 percent . . . with 42.7 percent of all Black children under eighteen officially classified as poor."

Since many believe, and so do I, that children's success in school is largely a function of economic and social stability in the family, family intervention to benefit the learning and development of children emerged about twenty-five yeras ago as an important family policy area (Weiss and Jacobs, 1988). It was thought that family programs for the poor that supported educational and, therefore, occupational attainment would be a means of tackling perceived national social problems (Moynihan, 1986).

Many programs, however, were based on a false set of assumptions, a number of which have been ably discussed in this volume. I have also recently catalogued some of these erroneous assumptions as they are presumed characteristic of Black communities (Slaughter, 1988): early intellectual deficit, deviant sex-role socialization, self-hatred and low self-esteem, and familial weakness and disorganization. In this volume, Miller-Jones and Spencer critically evaluate the first and third assumptions. With regard to the first, it is important to reemphasize the absence of evidence that Black infants are intellectually deficient, on average, at birth or during the first eighteen months of life (Freedman and DeBoer, 1979). As I have previously indicated (Slaughter, 1983), the purpose of educational intervention with Black children is to ensure that the children remain developmentally on course after the first eighteen months of life. With regard to the third assumption, we know that when Black parents deliberately teach children about the positive aspects of their heritage, children are more likely to have positive, pro-Black racial attitudes (Spencer, 1983), to have more adaptive racial coping strategies themselves as middle school–age children (Johnson, 1987), and to report having higher academic grades as adolescents (Bowman and Howard, 1985).

Today, we also know that family structure is not a reliable indicator of family functioning (Harrison, Serafica, and McAdoo, 1984; Hill, 1972). Despite socioeconomic status, the extended and/or augmented family is an important and continuing cultural influence in the Black child's socialization (Stack, 1974; Martin and Martin, 1978; Peters, 1978; McAdoo, 1981; Slaughter and Dilworth-Anderson, 1988). Fathers and mothers have historically been comfortable in sharing the nurturant, expressive dimensions of child care; girls have been encouraged to be assertive, and boys have not been taught that helping with household chores is unfeminine (Lewis, 1975). We need more basic research on child care and development within contemporary Black families to learn more of how these childhood competencies are optimally encouraged in natural urban settings. Clark's study (1983) of the family factors associated with higher- and lower-achieving Black adolescent youth in one- and two-parent poor families is an excellent example. We have learned that in order to design and implement effective family programs, this type of qualitative, process-oriented information is an essential complement to more quantitative, survey research.

The family, however, cannot perform the educative functions of the school. Nor can preschool educational intervention programs compensate for the school's responsibility to teach children. We know this now. Optimal schooling environments ensure developmental continuity between the preschool and the later school years (Slaughter and Epps, 1987). An essential component of those environments is cooperative relations between parents and teachers, relations that are decidedly at risk for many reasons in impoverished, culturally different communities. Furthermore, today many question whether schooling per se can ever be the principal route out of poverty (see Slaughter, Washington, Oyemade, and Lindsey, 1988). However these important issues are resolved, clearly research indicates that poverty in Black communities, from a developmental perspective, does not automatically connote weakness, pathological problems, deficit, or deviance in those communities, their families, or their children.

Conclusion

We are entering an era of renewed American concern for impoverished children and families. Recently, for example, the Committee on Child Development and Public Policy of the National Academy of Sciences devoted a considerable part of its agenda to consideration of children in poverty (April 28-29, 1988, and October 14-15, 1988). Given contemporary realities, and thanks to the Select Committee on Children, Youth, and Families, the concern is likely to be bipartisan. However, the coming era should benefit from the earlier refutations and challenges to myths and stereotypes about poor children and families, largely based on developmental research with Black children. The crucial question is whether poverty, especially Black poverty, is qualitatively different now than in earlier years. Although it may be worse (for example, the increasing numbers of single-parent families who are homeless), in every situation we can identify individuals who cope effectively and are remarkably resilient. Therefore, if developmental researchers continue to study these issues and if they adopt the newer perspectives as necessary points of departure, I believe that the results will more closely approximate the truth about Black communities, families, and children.

References

Bowman, P., and Howard, C. "Race-Related Socialization, Motivation, and Academic Achievement: A Study of Black Youth in Three-Generation Families." *Journal of the American Academy of Child Psychiatry*, 1985, *24* (2), 134-141.

Bronfenbrenner, U. "The War on Poverty: Won or Lost? America's Children on Poverty: 1959-1985." *Division of Child, Youth, and Family Services Newsletter*, 1986, *9* (3), 2-3.

Clark, R. *Family Life and School Achievement: Why Poor Black Children Succeed or Fail.* Chicago: University of Chicago Press, 1983.

Corcoran, M., Duncan, G., Gurin, G., and Gurin, P. "Myth and Reality: The Causes and Persistence of Poverty." *Journal of Policy Analysis and Management*, 1985, *4* (4), 516-536.

Davis, A. *Social-Class Influences upon Learning.* Cambridge, Mass.: Harvard University Press, 1948.

Davis, A., and Dollard, J. *Children of Bondage.* New York: Harper & Row, 1964. (Originally published 1940.)

Edelman, M. W. *Families in Peril: An Agenda for Social Change.* Cambridge, Mass.: Harvard University Press, 1987.

Elder, G. *Children of the Great Depression.* Chicago: University of Chicago Press, 1974.

Elder, G., Van Nguyen, T., and Caspi, A. "Linking Family Hardship to Children's Lives." *Child Development*, 1985, *56*, 361-375.

Freedman, D., and DeBoer, M. "Biological and Cultural Differences in Early Child Development." *Annual Review of Anthropology*, 1979, *8*, 579-600.

Harrison, A., Serafica, F., and McAdoo, H. "Ethnic Families of Color." In R. Parke (ed.), *Review of Child Development Research. VII: The Family.* Chicago: University of Chicago Press, 1984.

Hill, R. *The Strengths of Black Families.* New York: Emerson-Hall, 1972.

Johnson, D. "Identity Formation and Racial Coping Strategies of Black Children and Their Parents: A Stress and Coping Paradigm." Doctoral dissertation, Northwestern University, 1987.

Lewis, D. "The Black Family: Socialization and Sex Roles." *Phylon*, 1975, *35* (3), 221-237.

McAdoo, H. *Black Families.* Newbury Park, Calif.: Sage, 1981.

McLoyd, V. C., and Randolph, S. M. "The Conduct and Publication of Research on Afro-American Children: A Content Analysis." *Human Development*, 1984, *27*, 65-75.

Martin, E., and Martin, J. *The Black Extended Family.* Chicago: University of Chicago Press, 1978.

Moynihan, D. *The Negro Family: The Case for National Action.* Washington, D.C.: Office of Policy Planning and Research, U.S. Department of Labor, 1965.

Moynihan, D. *Family and Nation.* San Diego: Harcourt Brace Jovanovich, 1986.

Pearce, D., and McAdoo, H. *Women and Children Alone and in Poverty.* Washington, D.C.: National Advisory Council on Economic Opportunity, 1981.

Peters, M. (ed.). "Black Families." *Journal of Marriage and the Family*, 1978, *40* (4), entire issue.

Ramey, C. "Children and Public Policy: A Role for Psychologists." *American Psychologist*, 1974, *29* (1), 14-18.

Reppucci, N. D. "Psychology and the Public Interest." In A. Rogers and C. Scheier (eds.), *The G. Stanley Hall Lecture Series*. Vol. 5. Washington, D.C.: American Psychological Association, 1985.

Reppucci, N. D., and Kirk, R. "Psychology and Public Policy." In G. McCall and G. Weber (eds.), *Social Science and Public Policy: The Roles of Academic Disciplines in Policy Analysis*. Port Washington, N.Y.: Associated Faculty Press, 1984.

Ryan, W. *Blaming the Victim*. New York: Random House, 1971.

Slaughter D. T. "Early Intervention and Its Effects upon Maternal and Child Development." *Monographs of the Society for Research in Child Development*, 1983, *48* (4), entire issue.

Slaughter, D. T. "Programs for Racially and Ethnically Diverse American Families: Some Critical Issues." In H. Weiss and F. Jacobs (eds.), *Evaluating Family Programs*. Hawthorne, N.Y.: Aldine, 1988.

Slaughter, D. T., and Dilworth-Anderson, P. "Care of Black Children with Sickle Cell Disease: Fathers, Maternal Support, and Esteem." *Family Relations*, 1988, *37*, 281-287.

Slaughter, D. T., and Epps, E. G. "The Home Environment and Academic Achievement of Black American Children and Youth: An Overview." *Journal of Negro Education*, 1987, *56* (1), 3-20.

Slaughter, D. T., and McWorter, G. A. "Social Origins and Early Features of the Scientific Study of Black American Children and Families." In M. B. Spencer, G. K. Brookins, and W. R. Allen (eds.), *Beginnings: The Social and Affective Development of Black Children*. Hillsdale, N.J.: Erlbaum, 1985.

Slaughter, D. T., Washington, V., Oyemade, U., and Lindsey, R. "Head Start: A Backward and Forward Look." *Social Policy Report*. Washington, D.C.: Society for Research in Child Development, Washington Liaison Office, 1988.

Spencer, M. B. "Children's Cultural Values and Parental Child-Rearing Strategies." *Developmental Review*, 1983, *3*, 351-370.

Stack, C. *All Our Kin: Strategies for Survival in a Black Community*. New York: Harper & Row, 1975.

Swinton, D. "Economic Status of Blacks 1987." In J. Dewart (ed.), *The State of Black America 1988*. New York: National Urban League, 1988.

Wagner, D. "Child Development Research and the Third World." *American Psychologist*, 1986, *41* (3), 298-301.

Weiss, H., and Jacobs, F. *Evaluating Family Programs*. Hawthorne, N.Y.: Aldine, 1988.

Diana T. Slaughter is associate professor in the Human Development and Social Policy Program of the School of Education and Social Policy at Northwestern University. She is currently a member of the Committee on Child Development Research and Public Policy of the National Research Council, National Academy of Sciences, and of the Board of Ethnic and Minority Affairs of the American Psychological Association.

Index

A

Aboud, F. E., 64, 70
Achievement motivation, cultural diversity, in 14-15
African-American children. *See* Black children
Aid to Families with Dependent Children (AFDC), 7, 99, 100-101
Alejandro-Wright, M. N., 65, 66, 67, 70
Allen, W. R., 31, 41, 68, 72
American Psychiatric Association, 63, 70
American Psychological Association, 110, 112
Applebee, A., 38, 40
Au, K. U., 23, 25
Austin, G. A., 78, 90

B

Baillargeon, R., 83, 90
Banks, W. C., 64, 65, 70
Baratz, J. C., 86, 90
Barnes, E., 67, 70
Bartlett, E., 6, 43, 58
Bates, E., 50, 57
Baugh, J., 29, 40
Baumrind, D., 18, 25
Bendebba, M., 43, 50, 57
Bereiter, C., 86, 90, 97, 103
Berlin, B., 79, 90
Bernstein, B., 43-44, 56, 57
Birns, B., 81, 90
Black children: conclusion on, 114-115; cultural diversity, 20-21, 22-24; and developmental psychology reformulations, 75-92; educational interventions for, 109-116; and family context for learning, 30-33; identity development of, 65-68; information requests by, 51-56; language socialization for, 29-41; of middle- and working-class families, 30, 33-38; persistent poverty of, 2-3, 93, 99, 103, 112, 113; psychosocial impact of poverty on, 3-5; research and policy impacts of, 73-105; self-concept development by, 59-72; and social policy, 93-105; status of, as indicator, 5
Black English vernacular (BEV), and language socialization, 29, 34, 36-37
Black Family Summit, 39, 40
Black underclass, 1
Blau, Z. S., 31, 40
Bowler, M. K., 100, 104
Bowman, P., 67, 70, 113, 115
Boyce, C. M., 83-84, 90
Boykin, A. W., 23, 25
Brand, E. S., 64, 70
Brandis, W., 44, 57
Breedlove, D. E., 79, 90
Brice-Heath, S., 5-6, 29, 41
Bronfenbrenner, U., 31, 40, 76, 89, 90, 112, 115
Brookins, G. K., 31, 41, 68, 72
Brown v. Board of Education, 77, 101, 104
Bruner, J. S., 12, 17, 26, 50, 56, 57, 78, 81, 90

C

Campbell, E. Q., 104
Camras, L. A., 43, 57
Carey, S., 83, 84, 90
Carnegie Corporation of New York, 43*n*
Carroll, D. W., 49, 57
Case, R., 78, 90
Case Studies in Education and Culture, 31
Caspi, A., 112, 115
Castenada, A., 23, 27
Castenell, L., 65, 71
Cazden, C. B., 38, 40, 45, 57
Change: cultural diversity and development related to, 18-19; and language socialization, 38-40

Chesterfield, R., 17, 27
Child rearing: and cultural diversity, 17; and self-concept, 67, 69
Children. *See* Black children
Children's Defense Fund, 93, 97, 99, 104
Chomsky, N., 78, 86, 90
Ciborowski, T. J., 15, 25
Clark, D. H., 82, 91
Clark, K. B., 65, 77, 90
Clark, R., 114, 115
Cleveland, Ohio, extended family case in, 101
Cognitive competencies, cultural diversity in, 15-16, 23-24
Cognitive development: changed views of, 78-87; cross-cultural research on, 84-85; and information requests, 45-47; and intelligence, 80-84; and language development, 85-87
Cognitive environment, reconceptualized, 87-88
Cohen, R., 15, 25
Cohen, Y. A., 11, 25
Cole, M., 15, 19, 25, 26, 27-28, 32, 44, 56, 57, 58, 81, 85, 90, 92
Cole, O. J., 96, 104
Coleman, J. S., 38, 40, 97, 104
Committee of Correspondence on the Future of Public Education, 18, 26
Compensatory education, and social policy, 96-98
Competencies: acquiring, 16-17; cognitive, 15-16, 23-24; concept of, 12; and immigrants, 19, 21-22
Conflict resolution, and cultural diversity, 20
Congressional Budget Office (CBO), 2-3
Congressional Research Service (CRS), 2-3
Connolly, K. J., 12, 17, 26
Conti, D. J., 43, 57
Corcoran, M., 113, 115
Cross, W. E., Jr., 64, 65, 67, 70
Cross-cultural research: and cultural diversity, 14-15; in developmental psychology, 84-85
Cultural diversity: change and development related to, 18-19; and child rearing, 17; in cognitive competencies, 15-16, 23-24; concept of, 11-12; conclusion on, 24-25; and conflict resolution, 20; and cultural tasks, 13-16; and development, 11-28; formulas for, 16-18; and minority status, 19-24; primary and secondary, 21-24; and social policy, 100-101; in upward social mobility, 14-15
Cunningham, C. E., 94, 104

D

D'Andrade, R. G., 48, 57
Dasen, P., 13, 26
Davis, A., 109, 115
DeBoer, M., 113, 115
Development: change and cultural diversity related to, 18-19; concept of, 12; and cultural diversity, 11-28; cultural formulas for, 16-18; cultural influences on, 12; and cultural tasks, 13-16; of identity, 67-68; maturational or cultural outcomes of, 12-13; middle-class-centric view of, 16, 19, 21; and socialization, 9-72. *See also* Cognitive development
Developmental psychology: aspects of reformulating, 75-92; background on, 75-76; and cognitive environment, 87-88; and cognitive revolution, 78-87; conclusions on, 89-90; history of, 76-78; and information requests, 45-47; and social policy, 110-112
De Vos, G. A., 24, 26
Diagnostic and Statistical Manual (DSM-III), 63, 69
Dilworth-Anderson, P., 113, 116
Dines, J., 43, 58
Dockrell, J., 43, 58
Dollard, J., 109, 115
Dombrowski, J., 69, 71
Dore, J., 44, 48, 49, 56, 57
Dowley, G., 44, 56, 57
Duncan, G., 112, 113, 115

E

Edelman, M. W., 39, 40, 112, 115
Education: background on, 109-110;

and Black children, 109-116; compensatory, 96-98; and developmental psychology, 110-112; and identity process, 61-62, 64; interventions in, 112-114; and language socialization, 38-40, 45
Education Consolidation and Improvement Act, Chapter 1 of, 97
Edwards, R. M., 94, 104
Eells, K., 51, 58
Elder, G., 112, 115
Elementary and Secondary School Act, 96-97
Engelmann, S., 86, 90
Epps, E. G., 30, 41, 114, 116
Erickson, F., 16, 23, 26
Erikson, E., 68, 71
Erreich, A., 43, 57
Ervin-Tripp, S., 47, 58
Eurocentricity, and self-concept development, 63, 65, 66-67, 68
Evans, E. D., 60, 71
Examination questions, and language socialization, 47-48

F

Families: learning in, 30-33; middle- and working-class, 30, 33-38
Family Assistance Plan (FAP), 99, 100
Fanshel, D., 49, 50, 58
Farrar, M. J., 43, 58
Ferguson, C. A., 35, 41
Fifer, G., 82, 91
Fishbein, H. D., 12, 26
Folb, E. A., 30, 40
Follow-Through, 78, 97
Fordham, S., 24, 26
Freedle, R. O., 45, 57
Freedman, D., 113, 115
Freud, S., 63

G

Gardner, H., 83, 90
Garvey, C., 43, 50, 57
Gay, J., 15, 19, 25, 26
Gearhart, M., 45, 49, 57
Gelman, R., 83, 90
Gibson, M. A., 22, 26
Gilligan, C., 63, 71
Ginsburg, H., 13, 26, 81, 82, 90

Gladwin, T., 84-85, 90
Glasgow, D., 1, 7
Glick, J. A., 19, 25
Goffman, E., 49, 57
Golden, M., 81, 90
Goodnow, J. J., 78, 90
Gordon, R., 20, 28
Gordon, W., 15, 27
Gould, S. J., 79, 83, 90
Grant Foundation, W. T., 59n, 97, 105
Grice, H. P., 49, 57
Gumperz, J. J., 23, 26
Gurin, G., 113, 115
Gurin, P., 113, 115
Guthrie, L. F., 48, 56, 57

H

Hall, W. S., 6, 43, 44, 45, 46, 47, 48, 51, 56, 57, 58
Hamilton, C., 1, 7
Hamilton, D., 1, 7
Hare, B., 65, 71
Harrison, A., 113, 115
Hatcher, C. W., 39, 40
Head Start, 78, 94, 95, 96, 97, 102
Heath, S. B., 33, 35, 36, 38, 40
Henderson, D., 44, 57
Hess, R. D., 47, 56, 58, 86, 90
Hill, R., 101, 104, 114, 115
Hispanic children, poverty among, 3
Hobson, C. J., 104
Hoffer, T., 38, 40
Holt, G. S., 23, 26
Horowitz, F. D., 63, 66, 72
Howard, C., 67, 70, 113, 115
Hughes, A. T., 6, 43, 44, 45, 46, 58
Hunt, J. M., 81-82, 92
Hymes, D. H., 45, 57

I

Identity: concept of, 60-61; and reference group orientations, 66-68; understanding development of, 65-68
Identity formation, concept of, 61
Identity process: and self-concept development, 61-65; for sex role, 61, 63
Immigrants, and change of competencies, 19, 21-22

Information requests: aspects of, 43–58; assumptions about, 50–51; background on, 43–44; and cognitive and developmental psychology, 45–47; conclusion on, 55–56; and conversational turns, 53; findings on, 52–55; frequency of, 53–54; hypotheses on, 47–48; investigating, 51–52; and language socialization, 44–45; study method for, 48–51; types of, 54–55
Inner speech, role of, 46
Intelligence: reconceptualization of, 80–84; testing of, and social policy, 95

J

Jacobs, F., 113, 116
Jaeger, M. A., 20, 28
Jensen, A. R., 12, 26, 83, 90, 96, 97, 104
John, V. P., 45, 57
John-Steiner, V., 32
Johnson, D., 113, 115
Johnson, L. B., 94, 104
Johnson administration, 77–78
Jones, L. V., 97, 104

K

Kanuri, upward social mobility among, 14–15
Keil, F. C., 83, 84, 91
Kessel, F., 76, 89, 90
Kessen, W., 76, 89, 90
Kirk, R., 110, 116
Klee, T., 43, 58
Kochman, T., 23, 26
Kohn, M. L., 17, 26
Kuhn, D., 78, 91
Kuhn, T., 89, 91

L

Laboratory of Comparative Human Cognition, 78, 83, 84, 85, 91
Labov, W., 29, 40, 49, 50, 58, 86–87, 91
Lakatos, I., 89, 91
Lakoff, G., 79, 91
Language, development of, 85–97

Language socialization: aspects of, 29–41; background on, 29–30; concept of, 33; and education and preparing for change, 38–40; and expectations of children, 35–36; in families, 30–33; and information requests, 43–58; and judgments of competence of children, 37; in middle- and working-class families, 33–38; and primary language source, 34–35; and use of language for information, 36; and variants of language, 36–37
Laosa, L. M., 95, 97, 104
LaPoint, V., 101, 103, 105
Lave, C., 19, 27–28
Lave, J., 15, 26
Leacock, E. B., 17, 26
Leech, G., 50, 58
Lendon, R. J., 19, 27
Lesser, G. S., 82–83, 91, 92
Levine, L. W., 30, 41
LeVine, R. A., 11, 12, 26, 85, 92
Lewis, D., 114, 115
Lindsey, R., 114, 116
Linn, R., 47, 48, 58
Loosely, E. W., 17, 27

M

McAdoo, H. P., 66, 71, 93, 104, 112, 113, 115
McAdoo, J. L., 93, 104
McCandless, B. R., 60, 71
McCarthy, D., 85–86, 87, 91
McKechie, J., 43, 58
McLaughlin, M. W., 38, 40
McLoyd, V. C., 88, 91, 95, 98, 104, 110, 115
McPartland, J., 104
McWorter, G. A., 65, 71, 109, 110, 116
Martin, E., 113, 115
Martin, J., 113, 115
Maryland at College Park, University of, 43n
Mayer, P., 31, 41
Meacham, J. A., 82, 91
Meeker, M., 51, 58
Mehan, H., 44, 45, 58
Middle-class-centric view, of development, 16, 19, 21
Miller, G. A., 78, 91

Miller-Jones, D., 6, 75, 83, 91, 92, 95, 113
Minority: concept of, 2; status as, and cultural diversity, 19-24
Mirande, A., 94, 104
Mitchell, J., 96, 102, 104
Mitchell-Kernan, C., 47, 58
Moerk, E. L., 43, 58
Mohatt, G., 16, 23, 26
Mood, A. M., 104
Moroney, R. M., 101, 104
Moynihan, D. P., 2, 6, 7, 64, 65, 66, 68, 71, 93, 99-100, 104, 111, 112, 113, 115

N

Nagy, W. E., 44, 45, 47, 48, 57-58
National Academy of Sciences, Committee on Child Development and Public Policy of, 114
Native American children, and cultural diversity, 16, 22-24
Neilson, I., 43, 58
Neisser, U., 79, 83, 91
New York City, information requests study in, 51-56
Newell, A., 78, 91
Newman, D., 49, 57
Nigeria, upward social mobility in, 14-15
Ninio, A., 43, 49, 58
Nixon administration, 99-100
Nobles, W. W., 65, 71

O

Ochs, E., 32, 33, 35, 41
Office of Economic Opportunity, 94
Ogbu, J. U., 5, 11, 12, 17, 18, 21, 23, 24, 26-27, 28
Opper, S., 13, 26
Oppositional process, and minority status, 24
Osborn, D. K., 94, 104
Oyemade, U. J., 96, 105, 114, 116

P

Padilla, A. M., 64, 70
Pearce, D., 112, 113, 115
Perspectives on Human Deprivation Task Force, 79-80, 88
Peshkin, A., 31, 41

Peters, M., 113, 115
Philippines, upward social mobility in, 14
Philips, S. U., 16, 23, 27
Piaget, J., 13, 27, 67, 76, 78, 80, 81, 82, 86, 91-92
Pizzo, P., 95, 104
Plessy v. *Ferguson*, 77
Policy. *See* Social policy
Porter, J., 64, 65, 71
Posner, J., 15, 27
Poverty: Black children in, 2-3, 93, 99, 102, 112, 113; causes of, 1; and cognitive development, 79-80, 81-82, 84, 87-88; as deserved and undeserved, 100; and educational interventions, 112, 113, 114-115; psychosocial impact of, 3-5; and social policy, 93, 98-99, 103
Powell, G., 64, 71
Preschool development, and social policy, 95-96
Price-Williams, D. R., 15, 27
Problem solving, and language socialization, 46
Project Follow-Through, 78, 97
Project Head Start, 78, 94, 95, 96, 97, 101
Psychology. *See* Developmental psychology
Public assistance, and race, 98-99
Puluwat, and cross-cultural research, 84
Punjabi immigrants, and primary cultural differences, 21-22

R

Race: awareness of, and self-concept, 66; and social policy, 98-100
Ramey, C., 110, 116
Ramirez, M., 15, 23, 27
Randolph, S. M., 88, 91, 95, 98, 104, 110, 115
Raven, R. H., 79, 90
Reppucci, N. D., 110, 111, 116
Riddle, W. C., 97, 104
Riegel, K. F., 82, 92
Rogoff, B., 32, 41
Rosch, E., 79, 92
Rosenberg, M., 65, 71
Rosenfeld, J., 31, 41

Ruddle, K., 17, 27
Ruiz, R. A., 64, 70
Ryan, W., 1, 7, 111, 116

S

Samelson, F., 82, 92
Saxe, G. B., 15, 27
Schachter, F., 35, 41
Schieffelin, B. B., 32, 33, 35, 41
Scholnick, E. K., 44, 45, 46, 58
Scribner, S., 15, 19, 25, 27, 58, 85, 92
Seagrim, G. N., 19, 27
Seeley, J. R., 17, 27
Self-concept: in adolescence, 68–69; aspects of development of, 59–72; assumptions about, 60–61; background on, 59–60; and child rearing, 67, 69; concept of, 60; and identity development, 65–68; and identity process, 61–65; and policy considerations, 68–70; and race awareness, 66
Self-esteem: concept of, 60; and identity process, 64, 65–66
Semaj, L. T., 65, 66, 67, 71
Serafica, F., 113, 115
Shade, B. J., 23, 27
Sharp, D. W., 19, 25, 27–28
Shaw, J. C., 78, 91
Shipman, V., 47, 56, 58, 86, 90
Shure, M. B., 20, 28
Shweder, R. A., 85, 92
Simmons, R., 65, 71
Simon, H. A., 78, 91
Sims, H. A., 17, 27
Skerry, S. A., 64, 70
Slaughter, D. T., 30, 41, 65, 69, 71, 96, 104, 109, 110, 113, 114, 116
Smitherman, G., 30, 41
Snow, C. E., 35, 41
Social policy: aspects of, 93–105; background on, 93–94; competing interests in, 99–100; contributions of Black children to, 94–98; and cultural diversity, 100–101; and developmental psychology, 110–112; future for, 101–104; and race, 97–100
Socialization: and development, 9–72; models of, 31–32. *See also* Language socialization

Sosin, M., 1, 7
Spencer, M. B., 6, 31, 41, 59, 63, 64, 65, 66, 67, 68, 69, 71–72, 113, 116
Spencer Foundation, 59n
Spindler, G., 31
Spindler, L., 31
Spivack, G., 20, 28
Stack, C. B., 33, 41, 113, 116
Staples, R., 94, 104
Steiner, G. Y., 99, 105
Sternberg, R. J., 83, 92
Stevenson, H., 19, 28
Stodolsky, S. S., 82–83, 92
Super, C. M., 94, 105
Swinton, D., 113, 116
Szwed, J. F., 30, 41

T

Third World, culture change in, 18–19
Tomasello, M., 43, 58
Tulkin, S. R., 87, 92

U

U.S. Bureau of the Census, 102, 113
U.S. Department of Education, 97
U.S. Department of Health, Education, and Welfare, 4, 7, 79–80, 88, 92
U.S. House of Representatives: Committee on Ways and Means of, 2–3, 7; Select Committee on Children, Youth, and Families of, 3, 7, 114
U.S. Supreme Court, 77, 101
Upward social mobility, and cultural diversity, 14–15
Uzgiris, I. C., 81–82, 92

V

Van Nguyen, T., 112, 115
Vernon, P. E., 17, 18, 28
Vygotsky, L. S., 31–32, 41, 46, 58

W

Wachs, T. D., 81–82, 92
Wagner, D., 111, 116
War on Poverty, 77, 109
Ward, M. C., 31, 33, 41

Warner, W. L., 51, 58
Washington, R., 64, 71
Washington, V., 6-7, 93, 96, 99, 100, 101, 102, 103, 104, 105, 114, 116
Weinfeld, F. D., 104
Weiss, H., 113, 116
Wentworth, W. M., 32, 41
Wertsch, J. V., 32, 41, 46, 58, 76-77, 92
White, B. L., 16, 28
White, S., 76, 89, 90
White children: and cultural diversity, 14, 17, 20; information requests by, 51-56; poverty among, 3, 93, 99, 112
Whiting, B., 31, 41

Whiting, J., 31, 41
Whitten, N. E., Jr., 30, 41
Whorf, B. L., 86, 92
William T. Grant Foundation, 59n, 97, 105
Wilson, T. P., 43, 58
Wilson, W., 1, 7
Wish, M., 48, 57

Y

York, R. L., 104
Youniss, J., 76-77, 92

Z

Zimmerman, D. H., 43, 58

STATEMENT OF OWNERSHIP, MANAGEMENT AND CIRCULATION

1A. Title of Publication: New Directions for Child Development
1B. Publication No.: 4 9 4 - 0 9 0
2. Date of Filing: 10/26/88
3. Frequency of Issue: quarterly
3A. No. of Issues Published Annually: 4
3B. Annual Subscription Price: $45 indiv. / $60 inst.

4. Complete Mailing Address of Known Office of Publication:
350 Sansome Street, San Francisco, CA 94104

5. Complete Mailing Address of the Headquarters of General Business Offices of the Publisher:
350 Sansome Street, San Francisco, CA 94104

6. Full Names and Complete Mailing Address of Publisher, Editor, and Managing Editor

Publisher: Jossey-Bass Inc., Publishers, 350 Sansome Street, San Francisco, CA 94104

Editor: William Damon, Dept. of Psychology, Clark University, Worcester, MA 01610

Managing Editor: Allen Jossey-Bass, Jossey-Bass Inc., Publishers, 350 Sansome Street, San Francisco, CA 94104

7. Owner:

Full Name	Complete Mailing Address
Jossey-Bass Inc., Publishers	350 Sansome Street, San Francisco, CA 94104
for names and addresses of stockholders, see attached list	

8. Known Bondholders, Mortgagees, and Other Security Holders Owning or Holding 1 Percent or More of Total Amount of Bonds, Mortgages or Other Securities:

Full Name	Complete Mailing Address
same as #7	

10. Extent and Nature of Circulation

	Average No. Copies Each Issue During Preceding 12 Months	Actual No. Copies of Single Issue Published Nearest to Filing Date
A. Total No. Copies (Net Press Run)	1100	1175
B. Paid and/or Requested Circulation		
1. Sales through dealers and carriers, street vendors and counter sales	244	14
2. Mail Subscription (Paid and/or requested)	484	518
C. Total Paid and/or Requested Circulation	728	532
D. Free Distribution by Mail, Carrier or Other Means, Samples, Complimentary, and Other Free Copies	100	230
E. Total Distribution (Sum of C and D)	828	762
F. Copies Not Distributed		
1. Office use, left over, unaccounted, spoiled after printing	272	413
2. Return from News Agents		
G. TOTAL	1100	1175

11. I certify that the statements made by me above are correct and complete

Signature: [signed] Vice-President

PS Form 3526, Dec. 1987